73027

PS
1888
F62

Fogle

Hawthorne's imagery

Date Due

OC 1 7 '71	MAY 8 9 '9		
DE 13 '71			
DE 1 2 '72			
NO 3 0 '73			
FE 1 8 '74			
DEC 1 75			
OCT 10 '80			
MAR 21 '89			
OCT 0 4 '95			
NOV 1 8 '97			
DEC 1 1 '97			

HAWTHORNE'S IMAGERY

BY
RICHARD HARTER FOGLE

HAWTHORNE'S IMAGERY

THE
"PROPER LIGHT AND SHADOW"
IN THE MAJOR ROMANCES

UNIVERSITY OF OKLAHOMA PRESS
NORMAN

BY RICHARD HARTER FOGLE

Hawthorne's Imagery: The "Proper Light and Shadow" in the Major Romances (Norman, 1969)

Romantic Poets and Prose Writers (New York, 1967)

The Romantic Movement in American Writing (editor) (New York, 1966)

Hawthorne's Fiction: The Light & the Dark (Norman, 1952, 1964)

The House of the Seven Gables (editor) (New York, 1963)

The Idea of Coleridge's Criticism (Berkeley, 1962)

Eight American Writers (editor, with others) (New York, 1962)

Melville's Shorter Tales (Norman, 1960)

John Keats: Selected Poetry and Letters (New York, 1951)

The Imagery of Keats and Shelley (Chapel Hill, 1949)

STANDARD BOOK NUMBER: 8061–0855–X

LIBRARY OF CONGRESS CATALOG CARD NUMBER: 69–16723
COPYRIGHT 1969 BY THE UNIVERSITY OF OKLAHOMA PRESS,
PUBLISHING DIVISION OF THE UNIVERSITY. COMPOSED AND
PRINTED AT NORMAN, OKLAHOMA, U.S.A., BY THE UNIVER-
SITY OF OKLAHOMA PRESS. FIRST EDITION.

To Stephen Francis Fogle (1912-1967)
Fine scholar of Romanticism and great
teacher of literature.

Dilectissimē.

FOREWORD

THIS book supplements a previous volume, *Hawthorne's Fiction: The Light and the Dark* (1952; revised edition, 1964), and looks forward to a further work on Hawthorne and American and English Romanticism. It is narrower and more intensive than my earlier book; for the sake of a full demonstration of light-and-dark patterns, its scope is confined largely to the four major romances, *The Scarlet Letter*, *The House of the Seven Gables*, *The Blithedale Romance*, and *The Marble Faun*. I have not dealt with Hawthorne's tales, as I had originally planned and prepared to do, because my method of approach would have entailed very great length indeed, while on the other hand a summary chapter would have meant a greater shift of emphasis than I was willing to make. The early *Fanshawe*, while in many ways thoroughly representative of Hawthorne, proved irrelevant to my present purposes, as did the unfinished romances of the last phase, *The Ancestral Footstep*, *Septimius Felton*, *Dr. Grimshawe's Secret*, and *The Dolliver Romance*. Further, since despite their great interest and value Hawthorne's notebooks are not figurative as are his fictions, they have been disregarded. The sketch "Main Street" and various prefaces, however, lend themselves to discussion in terms of light-and-dark imagery and are appropriate to the romances and to Hawthorne's literary theory in general. It is, I trust, unnecessary to say that I have considerable acquaintance with the materials omitted.

My original intention was to deal with every aspect of the imagery of Hawthorne's fiction that I was capable of perceiving and composing in a coherent scheme, but I was deterred by persistent doubts about the desirability of this sort of completeness and about the digestibility of such an exposition. To intrude further upon the reader's patience in order to establish a context, I must add that I found myself returning to "the light and the dark," the theme of my earlier book, but now specifically in terms of image patterns, whereas I had previously worked toward total explications "in the round." It struck me increasingly that Hawthorne's use of light and darkness is central to his art and thought and that close attention to this one pattern would reveal reliable indications of the whole. The approach is limited; it is far from covering all the problems of prose fiction. Yet the limitation is part of its strength and serves to bring out a lyric intensity in Hawthorne which most have felt though none have defined.

My method of analysis is in one sense old-fashioned. It grants to Hawthorne his *donnée* of illusion, attributing to his characters the three-dimensional reality of life. In this respect I have tried to be something like the ideal sympathetic reader that Hawthorne yearns for in his prefaces. At the same time I have everywhere implied, though without seeking to enforce it, an archetypal design in which the characters are single elements and symbols. Also, complying with Hawthorne's basic pictorial metaphor for his verbal art, I have treated his language not absolutely and in itself but only as medium, a "bright transparency" of the pictures it conveys. This approach is perhaps inevitable in an imagery study; it is also faithful to Hawthorne's own conception of his purposes, very close to the traditional *ut pictura poesis*. As a consequence, the method is much less complexly dialectical than it would be if I were dealing with language in itself and the "interinanimation of words": the dialectic is centered only in the central opposition of light and dark images. And this pattern of dialectical struggle, it should be noted, is further modified by the primacy given to sun imagery in the discussion.

While I have from time to time drawn explicit conclusions in this book, they are scattered here and there as they arise from their contexts. They are deliberately suggestive rather than definitive, and those that are set down in the "Afterword" (Chapter VII) are very brief. The reader will discern, I trust, a total and coherent design, but one to which he must supply his own emphasis. Though arranged and interpreted, the evidence—the concrete instances—stands in the foreground. The very few citations of previous scholarship and criticism are chiefly casual references to interesting recent work which I have scanned in the process of writing, such as Terence Martin's *Hawthorne* and Bruce Franklin's paperback edition of *The Scarlet Letter and Other Writings by Nathaniel Hawthorne*.

I can fairly claim a general grasp of Hawthorne scholarship. The present work is intended to be a part of this scholarship and a contribution to it. Thus I am indebted to such early critics as Edwin P. Whipple, George P. Lathrop, Henry James, and Anthony Trollope; to the seminal influence of F. O. Matthiessen's great *American Renaissance*; to the sensitivity of Newton Arvin; to Hyatt Howe Waggoner's *Hawthorne* and Roy R. Male's *Hawthorne's Tragic Vision*, akin though quite independent of my own thinking; to the careful and comprehensive studies of Arlin Turner; and to many another.

In this connection it is well to speak of the relation of the present enterprise to literary history. As one of the first modern students of Hawthorne to deal directly with his texts, I would emphatically deprecate any absolute distinction between the critical approach and the historical one. In reviewing the first edition of *Hawthorne's Fiction*, Randall Stewart, most eminent of Hawthorne scholars, remarked with urbane astonishment that I was evidently writing *sub specie aeternitatis*, since no date was anywhere to be found in the book. The truth is, however, that it aspired neither to the splendors of the absolute nor to the miseries of isolation. It relied implicitly upon Hawthorne biography, Hawthorne's notebooks (including Stewart's own notable editions), and in general upon a historical conception of his period and environment. My desire to study Hawthorne's work in itself was not intended to deny to it the larger contexts within which it subsisted.

On the other hand, a wrong application of literary history would leave this work no self or would impose an impenetrable barrier to keep us from reaching it. The critic as I conceive him has no quarrel with literary history per se; but when it becomes so deterministic or so abstract that it dissolves his subject into something else, or diminishes it into something too small to see, he must perforce cast about him for room to operate. And if a critic is required to review at length the possible considerations of historical, cultural, and biographical environment that might conceivably bear upon his writer's work, it is unlikely that he will ever get to his proper subject at all.

Criticism, as it is thought of here, involves a fusion of author and critic and a reconciliation of universal principles with the temporal relativism of history. The critic strives to state objectively what he sees, and part of his objectivity lies in historical perspective. However, both his limitation and his value lie in the fact that he is *interpreting*. His own beliefs, his own point of view, inevitably dictate what he will see. His individuality is also his vitality, as long as his main object is still the work that he expounds. Good literary historians, such as Hubert H. Hoeltje (*Inward Sky*) and Edward Wagenknecht (*Nathaniel Hawthorne*), have sought to restore Hawthorne wholly to the nineteenth century by reviving the full sense of his nineteenth-century attachments. The reminder is important for those who have forgotten them, but it ignores our reasons for reading him in the twentieth.

Historical considerations lead one to reject depth psychology, especially Freudian psychology, as a major issue in Hawthorne. Frederick Crews's recent *The Sins of the Fathers* apparently regards avoidance of it as not merely misguided but positively dishonest; Crews is so vigorous in his utterance, expressed in a substantial book, that, although the topic does not lie directly in my way, I would seem lacking in candor to pass it by.

Yet to me, despite the cogent arguments of Lionel Trilling, Frederick Hoffman, and others, the Freudian remains the least attractive of psychological approaches. The application of depth psychology is permissible in interpretation if it is employed metaphorically to express an added dimension or overtone of meaning, though the Freudian metaphors and symbols are abstract, crudely analogical, and in general unlovely. If the Freudian system is taken as a literal scientific truth, then it supplants rather than explains the fiction that is thought to be harboring it. One looks, as it were, through the manifest content of the dream of art to search out the latent content beneath it and concealed by it. But art *is* the manifest content, and it is to be looked *at*, not *through*.

One cannot, of course, rigidly deny the application of Freudian theory to pre-Freudian literature—though one might reflect of Sophocles' Oedipus, as opposed to Cocteau's: "O Oedipus, unhappiest of men, and scourged by the gods, amid your dire afflictions you were spared one ill. At least you never had an Oedipus complex." As for sexual implications, we must concede not only that sex is here to stay but also that it has been around all the time. One wonders, however, whether the Freudian critic takes sufficient account of the possibility that men have at all times been aware of the fact and have not always felt the moral obligation of discussing it as the source of human actions. In the case of Hawthorne, convention obviously made it impossible to discuss it openly, but there is little evidence that he desired to do so or even conceived of the possibility of doing so. With reference to Crews's book, which is concerned with guilt or guilt feelings, Hawthorne's fiction is much preoccupied with guilt: the dream motif is frequent in it, his phrase "psychological romance" suggests dark explorations, and he remarks in *The House of the Seven Gables* that the legend of today may well become the psychological science of tomorrow. However, these aspects are parts and not the whole of his work by any means.

The formulations and terminology of depth psychology alter the imagination itself in those conversant with it. And, to speak only of the nineteenth century, to think of Hawthorne, Melville, Wordsworth, Coleridge, or Tennyson primarily as unconscious prophets of a new psychological dispensation is to take leave of them as literary artists, and to take leave of literary criticism as well. Hawthorne's fiction does not sound like this; and allowing for all the dynamic implications it may contain of the promptings of the unconscious, it does not have the clinical spirit, nor is it a form of therapy. Morality is Hawthorne's theme as well as psychological exploration; his characters are held to be responsible persons who possess freedom of will. If, dissatisfied with this, we proceed by metaphysics toward the ultimate mysteries of free will and determinism—however we may sympathize and palliate, grow fascinated with the dark treasure in the interior of Dimmesdale's heart or the great red ruby of Miriam's guilt—in Hawthorne the simple supposition of moral responsibility still holds.

For quotations from *The Scarlet Letter* and *The Marble Faun*, I have used the Houghton Mifflin Riverside editions of the 1880's. *The House of the Seven Gables* is cited from Hyatt Howe Waggoner's text of 1964 in the new Riverside Editions; and *The Blithedale Romance*, from the current Ohio State University Centenary Edition.

RICHARD HARTER FOGLE

Chapel Hill
January 15, 1969

CONTENTS

HAWTHORNE'S IMAGERY

"Pray, oblige me by removing to this other bench, and I venture to assure you the proper light and shadow will transform the spectacle into quite another thing."

NATHANIEL HAWTHORNE, "Main Street"

I. THE PREFACES AND
OTHER CRITICISM

IN a famous passage of his 1851 Author's Preface to *Twice-Told Tales*, Hawthorne remarks that the stories

> have the pale tint of flowers that blossomed in too retired a shade,—the coolness of a meditative habit, which diffuses itself through the feeling and observation of every sketch. ... The book, if you would see anything in it, requires to be read in the clear, brown, twilight atmosphere in which it was written; if opened in the sunshine, it is apt to look exceedingly like a volume of blank pages.

This is one of the most discouraging of Hawthorne's invariably disparaging self-criticisms; nevertheless, it is a good place to begin a discussion that intends to emphasize images of light and darkness and their relationships.

First, the passage does implicate light, even if only by negation. Next, the underlying figure is pictorial; and, in fact, in the Preface Hawthorne continually refers to the *Twice-Told Tales* as "sketches." The caution about the atmosphere in which the book "requires to be read" implies, too, a regard for harmony, appropriateness, "keeping," a kind of reconciliation that is re-echoed in the final reflection concerning the tales' effect upon their author: "... his pleasant pathway among realities seems to proceed out of the Dreamland of his youth, and to be bordered with just enough of its shadowy foliage to shelter him from the heat of the day." In Hawthorne, light needs to be modified, or, as the case may be, accentuated, by shadow; heat, tempered with coolness; reality, relieved by a Something Else that will vary according to the reality opposed.

Thus, in the earlier "Old Manse" essay, the period of the *Mosses* is a "fairyland" where "there is no measurement of time," where "three years hastened away a noiseless flight, as the breezy sunshine chases the cloud shadows across the depths of a still valley," and the charm of the book is inseparable from "the sunshine glimmering through the willow branches while I wrote." It should be observed that the instances cited here suggest transience as well as the harmony they were adduced to illustrate. Hawthorne frequently reaches out toward synthesis and totality, but the gesture is always tentative. He never commits himself to a single image, a single picture, a single mood. There is in him the sense of a consummate whole, but one only ideally attainable, never to be realized concretely. Fullness is perhaps conceivable as a moving panorama, or even as a globe that can be turned before one on its axis; but it can be only perceived in the aspect immediately presented, not grasped as unity.

Thus the experience of the Custom House was useful, but it was something to be stored up for later application; it could not include the experience it supplanted:

4

I took it in good part, at the hands of Providence, that I was thrown into a position so little akin to my past habits, and set myself seriously to gather from it whatever profit was to be had. . . . I look upon it as an evidence, in some measure, of a system naturally well balanced, and lacking no essential part of a thorough organization, that, with such associates to remember, I could mingle at once with men of altogether different qualities, and never murmur at the change.

Yet, "A gift, a faculty if it had not departed, was suspended and inanimate within me." The experience was not in itself complete: "I never considered it as other than a transitory life. There was always a prophetic instinct, a low whisper in my ear, that, within no long period, and whenever a new change of custom should be essential to my good, a change would come."

Hawthorne's most comprehensive image of artistic creation, or rather the most favorable condition for artistic creation, was illuminated by moonlight and firelight. He avowed that in the atmosphere of the Custom House "my imagination was a tarnished mirror. It would not reflect, or only with miserable dimness, the figures with which I did my best to people it." Nor was the case better with him even "when, late at night, I sat in the deserted parlor, lighted only by the glimmering coal-fire and the moon, striving to picture forth imaginary scenes, which, the next day, might flow out on the brightening page in many-hued description."

The ensuing passage has been quoted very frequently and sometimes interpreted at length. In exhibiting it once more, I can only plead its great richness and its peculiar aptness to my subject:

> If the imaginative faculty refused to act at such an hour, it might well be deemed a hopeless case. Moonlight, in a familiar room, falling so white upon the carpet, and showing all its figures so distinctly—making every object so minutely visible, yet so unlike a morning or noontide visibility,—is a medium the most suitable for a romance-writer to get acquainted with his illusive guests.

Moonlight was for Hawthorne peculiarly the light of imagination, though seldom sufficient in itself. The *distinctness* of the figures of the carpet also had a special significance, for distinctness was to him an attribute of reality, the vision of which was very precious to him, very hard to gain, and tragically easy to lose. This clarity of outline was in partial opposition to the illusiveness that moonlight and imagination implied.

The furnishings of the chamber represented the known and familiar:

> There is the little domestic scenery of the well-known apartment; the chairs, with each its separate individuality; the centre-table, sustaining a work-basket, a volume or two, and an extinguished lamp; the sofa; the bookcase; the picture on the wall,—all these details, so completely seen, are so spiritualized by the unusual light, that they seem to lose their actual substance, and become things of intellect.

Much might be said here about the relation of this effect to Romantic doctrines of the imagination and of the picturesque, but for present purposes it is enough to note the distinctness and individuality of the objects seen and, conversely, their transmutation into pure meaning and symbol, "spiritualized by the unusual light." Summarized, the usual and unusual, the familiar and the strange, are fused in the vision:

> Nothing is too small or too trifling to undergo this change, and acquire dignity thereby. A child's shoe; the doll, seated in her little wicker carriage; the hobby-horse,—whatever, in a word, has been used or played with, during the day, is now invested with a quality of strangeness and remoteness, though still almost as vividly present as by daylight.

"Thus, therefore," Hawthorne continues, "the floor of our familiar room has become a neutral territory, somewhere between the real world and fairy-land, where the Actual and the Imaginary may meet, and each imbue itself with the nature of the other." Plainly the moonlight stands for the Imaginary; the familiar objects and associations, for the Actual; and their meeting, at once weird and matter-of-fact, provides artistic illusion:

> Ghosts might enter here, without affrighting us. It would be too much in keeping with the scene to excite surprise, were we to look about us and discover a form beloved, but gone hence, now sitting quietly in a streak of this magic moonshine, with an aspect that would make us doubt whether it had returned from afar, or had never once stirred from our fireside.

This "neutral territory" is Hawthorne's central formulation for romance, as Terence Martin has recently re-emphasized; but there is a further component to be considered, another light:

The somewhat dim coal-fire has an essential influence in producing the effect which I would describe. It throws its unobtrusive tinge throughout the room, with a faint ruddiness upon the walls and ceiling, and a reflected gleam from the polish of the furniture. This warmer light mingles itself with the cold spirituality of the moonbeams, and communicates, as it were, a heart and sensibilities of human tenderness to the forms which fancy summons up. It converts them from snow-images into men and women.

In a further perspective, "Glancing at the looking-glass, we behold—deep within its haunted verge—the smouldering glow of the half-extinguished anthracite, the white moonbeams on the floor, and a repetition of all the gleam and shadow of the picture, with one remove further from the actual, and nearer to the imaginative." The passage presents the ideal setting for imaginative creation: "Then, at such an hour, and with this scene before him, if a man, sitting all alone, cannot dream strange things, and make them look like truth, he need never try to write romances."

The scene is a single image, but, as is evident, it is easily divisible into its component parts. The moonlight of imagination is primary; it does not, however, include the other elements but is supplemented by them. By itself it could produce only snow images. The combination of the familiar with the unusual is central to the Romanticism of Coleridge and Wordsworth, as is also the preservation of individuality in the objects that the moonlight transforms —this is the Romantic conception of the picturesque. Hawthorne, preoccupied with maintaining reality, emphasizes the distinctness of the "figures," their "minute visibility," as we shall see more than once later on. The combination of light and object, unusual and familiar, presents the ideal symbol of Romantic art, in a fusion of meaning and form: "All these details, so completely seen, are so spiritualized by the unusual light, that they seem to lose their actual substance, and become things of intellect."

Yet, having achieved this result, Hawthorne nevertheless continues with the "warmer light" of the fire, which "mingles itself with the cold spirituality of the moonbeams," and the further element of the looking glass of ideal imitation, "with one remove further from the actual" in its "repetition of all the gleam and shadow of the picture." In other words, he conceives a synthesis but presents it in its parts, moving them past us one by one, as each suggests still other elements of a total process. Indeed, the ideal process and result that he envisions, the full synthesis of Actual and Imaginary, is not possible to him at all, a fact that he understands while holding himself morally responsible for it.

The pressure of the Actual is too heavy for the creation of romance: "But, for myself, during the whole of my Custom House experience, moonlight and sunshine, and the glow of firelight, were just alike in my regard; and neither of them was of one whit more avail than the twinkle of a tallow-candle." The next sentence is crucial: "An entire class of susceptibilities, and a gift connected with them,—of no great richness or value, but the best I had,—was gone from me." The synthesis that is theoretically possible, "to diffuse thought and imagination through the opaque substance of to-day, and thus to make it a bright transparency; to spiritualize the burden that began to weigh so heavily; to seek, resolutely, the true and

9

indestructible value that lay hidden in the petty and weari-
some incidents, and ordinary characters, with which I was
not conversant," is a counsel of impossible perfection for
Hawthorne, although he avows that the fault is his. Perhaps we should bear in mind that what he did go on to
write was *The Scarlet Letter*.

Bruce Franklin, maintaining that "Hawthorne displays
history as a public revelation and manifestation of private
psychological disease," finds the showman of the sketch
"Main Street" (in *The Snow-Image and Other Twice-
Told Tales*) at least partly diabolical in his use of artistic
illusion, his "lighting effects" (see Franklin's introduction
to *The Scarlet Letter and Other Writings by Nathaniel
Hawthorne*). This interesting notion is true, I think, only
in a special sense and as a possibility. I am concerned here,
however, with the artistic illusion itself, primarily in terms
of light and darkness. The showman is Hawthorne himself, who intends to exhibit "more than two centuries" of
Salem history in a "shifting panorama," to illustrate "the
march of time." Thus he has figuratively contrived "a certain pictorial exhibition, somewhat in the nature of a
puppet-show, by means of which I propose to call up the
multiform and many-colored Past . . . with no greater
trouble than the turning of a crank."

The showman's art presents itself immediately, then,
skeptically and unfavorably as a contrived illusion. In the
sketch as a whole, the Indian aborigines of the territory
are associated with darkness; the whites who supplant them,
with light—matter of factly, because it is their function to
clear the dark forests for civilized settlements. The present, which the showman significantly does not attain be-

cause his crank breaks down, is conceived as broad day-light. For his exhibition he claims harmony and keeping:

> The little wheels and springs of my machinery have been well oiled; a multitude of puppets are dressed in character, representing all varieties of fashion, from the Puritan cloak and jerkin to the latest Oak Hall coat; the lamps are trimmed, and shall brighten into noontide sunshine, or fade away in moonlight, or muffle their brilliancy in a November cloud, as the nature of the scene may require.

At the beginning Main Street is a "hardly perceptible track," traversed at one point by "a little streamlet, which glitters like a snake through the gleam of sunshine, and quickly hides itself among the underbrush." Here we discern "the great Squaw Sachem" and "Wappacowet, her second husband, the priest and magician, whose incantations shall hereafter affright the pale-faced settlers with grisly phantoms, dancing and shrieking in the woods at midnight." Wappacowet, himself an artistic illusionist, supports Franklin's argument for the semidiabolic character of the showman: "But greater would be the affright of the Indian necromancer, if, mirrored in the pool of water at his feet, he could catch a prophetic glimpse of the noonday marvels which the white man is destined to achieve." At present, however, the Squaw Sachem and Wappacowet

> pass on, beneath the tangled shade, holding high talk on matters of state and religion. . . . the gloom of the broad wilderness impends over them, and its sombre mystery invests them as with something preternatural; and only momentary streaks of quivering sunlight, once in a great

while, find their way down, and glimmer among the feathers in their dusky hair.

The advent of the white man is signalized by "an upheaved axe . . . glittering in the sunshine." The dwelling of the first settler, Roger Conant,

> is surrounded by a cleared space of a few acres, where Indian corn grows thrivingly among the stumps of the trees; while the dark forest hems it in, and seems to gaze silently and solemnly, as if wondering at the breadth of sunshine which the white man spreads around him. An Indian, half hidden in the dusky shade, is gazing and wondering too.

The forest track slowly grows more distinct: ". . . it goes onward from one clearing to another, here plunging into a shadowy strip of woods, there open to the sunshine, but everywhere showing a decided line, along which human interests have begun to hold their career." Meanwhile, "in its more secluded portions, . . . the black shadow of the forest strives to hide the trace of human footsteps."

In the midst of the exhibition, a critic, who has already spoken up earlier, protests the lifelessness of the display: " 'Here is a pasteboard figure, such as a child would cut out of a card, with a pair of very dull scissors.' " The showman defends himself: " 'But, sir, you have not the proper point of view. . . . You sit altogether too near to get the best effect of my pictorial exhibition. Pray, oblige me by removing to this other bench, and I venture to assure you the proper light and shadow will transform the spectacle into quite another thing.' " But the critic will have none of this. He replies: " 'Pshaw! . . . I want no other light and shade. I have already told you that it is my business to see things just as they are.' "

The showman continues, of course, despite the objections. How, he asks, could the Puritan forest settlers dispense with the impressive churches and cathedrals of their former worship; "how, with the pictured windows, where the light of common day was hallowed by being transmitted through the glorified figures of saints?" He answers himself, however, that "they needed nothing of all this . . . the zeal of a recovered faith burned like a lamp within their hearts, enriching everything around them with its radiance. . . . All was well, so long as their lamps were freshly kindled at the heavenly flame." Yet the question remains unsettled: "After a while, however, whether in their time or their children's, these lamps began to burn more dimly, or with a less genuine lustre; and then it might be seen how hard, cold, and confined was their system." Meanwhile, they spread light after their own fashion: "The wild forest is shrinking back," and "the tender and modest wildflowers, those gentle children of savage nature that grew pale beneath the ever-brooding shade, have shrunk away and disappeared, like stars that vanish in the breadth of light." As sturdier replacements, a little later came "men of history and legend, whose feet leave a track of brightness along any pathway which they have trodden."

At another interruption by the critic the showman mildly remonstrates that

"you break the illusion of the scene. But—merely for your own pleasure, sir—let me entreat you to take another point of view. Sit further back, by that young lady, in whose face I have watched the reflection of every changing scene; only oblige me by sitting there; and, take my word for it, the slips of pasteboard shall assume spiritual life, and the bedaubed canvas become an airy and changeable reflex of what it purports to represent."

However, the critic replies that " 'as for my own pleasure, I shall best consult it by remaining precisely where I am.' " The showman thus pleads for the conventions of art, the willing suspension of disbelief or poetic half-faith that it requires in its audience, while the critic is the Philistine, the Platonic detractor, the simple-minded realist—whom Hawthorne in moods of depression felt to be representative of the American public.

The showman feels the need for artistic foreshortening of the long span of Salem's history:

> It will be hardly worth our while to wait two, or it may be three, turnings of the hour-glass, for the conclusion of the lecture. Therefore, by my control over light and darkness, I cause the dusk, and then the starless night, to brood over the street; and summon forth again the bellman, with his lantern casting a gleam about his footsteps.

Indeed, most of the subsequent narrative is gloomy, portraying the spiritual and cultural decline of Puritanism over the course of the seventeenth century, culminating in the Salem witchcraft trials: "Such life was sinister to the intellect, and sinister to the heart; especially when one generation had bequeathed its religious gloom, and the counterfeit of its religious ardor, to the next." The showman apologizes:

> These scenes, you think, are all too sombre. So, indeed, they are; but the blame must rest on the sombre spirit of our

forefathers, who wove their web of life with hardly a single thread of rose-color or gold, and not on me, who have a tropic-love of sunshine, and would gladly gild all the world with it, if I knew where to find so much.

As the showman's attempts to relieve the "dreary monotony" of the scene, his machine breaks down.

The misfortune is great:

> The scenes to come were far better than the past. The street itself would have been more worthy of pictorial exhibition; the deeds of its inhabitants not less so. And how would your interest have deepened, as, passing out of the cold shadow of antiquity, in my long and weary course, I should arrive within the limits of man's memory, and, leading you at last into the sunshine of the present, should give a reflex of the very life that is flitting past us!

Indeed, the narrative might well have concluded in a blaze of glory:

> Then, too,—and it is what I chiefly regret,—I had expended a vast deal of light and brilliancy on a representation of the street in its whole length, from Buffum's Corner downward, on the night of the grand illumination for General Taylor's triumph.

This comment is of course ironic, and even bitterly ironic, since the triumph of Taylor and the Whigs banished Hawthorne from the Salem Custom House. One interpretation would be that what has been omitted is impossible as a subject for the artist, in addition to the probable ironies of Hawthorne's attitude toward the recent and contemporary history of Salem. Yet, on the other hand, we cannot afford to forget that the light of common day remained a problem to Hawthorne and that a little later, in the "Custom House" essay, he was to express a wish that he might make a "bright transparency" of the opaque substance of the actual. His subsequent prefaces expound and defend the romance, the methods of the artist of the picturesque, but in them actuality and its broad, commonplace sunshine is at once the great antagonist and the object of a vain desire.

In the Preface to *The Snow-Image and Other Twice-Told Tales*, Hawthorne describes himself as "burrowing, to his utmost ability, into the depths of our common nature, for the purposes of psychological romance," as one "who pursues his researches in that dusky region, as he needs must, as well by the tact of sympathy as by the light of observation." Reflecting upon his past career in writing, he asks:

> . . . was there ever such a weary delay in obtaining the slightest recognition from the public, as in my case? I sat down by the wayside of life, like a man under enchantment, and a shrubbery sprung up around me, and the bushes grew to be saplings, and the saplings became trees, until no exit appeared possible, through the entangling depths of my obscurity."

The comments have their relationship. The "light of observation" needs to be modified by the "tact of sympathy" for the dusky region of psychological romance. Likewise, Hawthorne's "depths of obscurity" have been an element in the harmonious keeping of his life, as he remarks in the Author's Preface to *Twice-Told Tales*: ". . . his pleasant pathway among realities seems to proceed out of the

Dreamland of his youth, and to be bordered with just enough of its shadowy foliage to shelter him from the heat of the day."

The same principle is enunciated in some famous sentences from the Preface to *The House of the Seven Gables*. The romancer may, if he thinks fit, "so manage his atmospherical medium as to bring out or mellow the lights and deepen and enrich the shadows of the picture." *The House of the Seven Gables*

> is the legend prolonging itself, from an epoch now gray in the distance, down into our own broad daylight, and bringing along with it some of its legendary mist, which the reader, according to his pleasure, may either disregard, or allow it to float almost imperceptibly about the characters and events for the sake of a picturesque effect.

The author has not chosen to mar the harmonies of his picturesque story by didacticism. He

> has considered it hardly worth his while, therefore, relentlessly to impale the story with its moral as with an iron rod,— or, rather, as by sticking a pin through a butterfly,—thus at once depriving it of life, and causing it to stiffen in an ungainly and unnatural attitude.

The "moral" may become itself an element of the harmony of the picturesque, by the gradations and interrelationships of its light: "A high truth, indeed, fairly, finely, and skilfully wrought out, brightening at every step, and crowning the final development of a work of fiction, may add an artistic glory. . . ."

These harmonies are lost upon the reader who refuses to adopt the right position from which to view them—or to understand that he is viewing a work of art with its own principles and laws. Like the critic in "Main Street," he interposes a hostile actuality. Thus Hawthorne regrets the closeness of *The House of the Seven Gables* to "an actual locality": "Not to speak of other objections, it exposes the romance to an inflexible and exceedingly dangerous species of criticism, by bringing his fancy-pictures almost into positive contact with the realities of the moment." Now, as has been intimated earlier, there is something of this critic in Hawthorne himself, or he would not feel his objections so strongly and so constantly. Whether the critic is located primarily in the writer or in the hostile environment of his America is an interesting question, but a question rather to be asked than to be answered, since its possible permutations and combinations are practically endless.

Hawthorne returns to the problem of actuality in the Preface to *The Blithedale Romance*. If *Blithedale* is to be treated as an imitation of actual events, places, and people, then "many readers will, probably, suspect a faint and not very faithful *shadowing* [italics mine] of BROOK FARM, in Roxbury, which (now a little more than ten years ago) was occupied and cultivated by a company of socialists." The author has indeed "occasionally availed himself of his actual reminiscences," but with a purpose that is artistic and pictorial, "in the hope of giving a more life-like tint to the fancy-sketch in the following pages." His "treatment of the affair [Brook Farm] is altogether incidental to the main purpose of the romance." The setting is, in the terms used in "The Custom House," "a neutral territory, somewhere between the real world and fairy-land, where the Actual and the Imaginary may meet, and each imbue itself with the nature of the other." Blithedale furnishes the neutral territory. Hawthorne's "present concern with the socialist community is merely to establish a theatre, a little removed from the highway of ordinary travel, where the creatures of his brain may play their phantasmagorical antics, without exposing them to too close a comparison with the actual events of real lives."

The American romancer has special problems. He is not permitted the "conventional privilege" accorded to the writer

> in the old countries, with which fiction has long been conversant . . . . Among ourselves, on the contrary, there is as yet no such Faery Land, so like the real world, that, in a suitable remoteness, one cannot well tell the difference, but with an atmosphere of strange enchantment, beheld through which the inhabitants have a propriety of their own.

Terence Martin has recently pointed out a weakness in this geographical figure: it is made objective and independent of the mind of the "romancer," whereas it is the romancer's responsibility to create it himself. The objection is cogent; consideration of it, however, leads to consideration of the mental process behind it. Hawthorne, one speculates, is using a dialectic to reconcile opposites (speculates, because there is no certainty of the order or the priority of time and importance in which the elements of the dialectic present themselves). There is the world of art—more specifically, the world of romance—and there is the world of actuality, each opposed to the other and each with legitimate claims to recognition. The "neutral territory" is, of course, the reconciliation between them. This is perhaps entirely obvious, but, as Martin's argument implies, Hawthorne has made his reconciliation difficult by making these worlds unusually solid, exclusive, and self-contained. The "neutral territory" is between them rather than of them; their own boundaries remain intact and apart. The result of their relationship, their reconciliation, the result that Hawthorne desires, is precarious; a "neutral territory" between separate states is not a very spacious ground.

Martin's further remark that Hawthorne's literary theory deals with the conditions of artistic creation rather than with the creation itself is also just, but I prefer not to make the distinction but to deal more loosely with the relations of the topic.

To return, then, to the neutral territory, or "Faery Land," of the romance: "This atmosphere is what the American romancer needs." Otherwise the hostile critic is in power. "In its absence, the beings of imagination are compelled to show themselves in the same category as actually living mortals; a necessity that generally renders the paint and pasteboard of their composition but too painfully discernible." Hawthorne is well aware of one solution to his problem, which is to give his world of romance absolute preference and autonomy, subject only to its own laws of harmony. As we have seen, however, this is a solution that he is unwilling to employ, though it is implicit in the passages now under discussion. Consequently:

With the idea of partially obviating this difficulty (the sense of which has always pressed very heavily upon him), the author has ventured to make free with his old and affectionately remembered home at BROOK FARM, as being certainly the most romantic episode of his own life,—essentially a day-dream, and yet a fact,—and thus offering an available foothold between fiction and reality. Furthermore, the scene was in good keeping with the personages whom he desired to introduce.

The laws to which the romancer might have appealed are glanced at in the phrase "good keeping," and in the earlier statement that "the inhabitants have a propriety of their own."

Italy is Hawthorne's "neutral territory" in the Preface to *The Marble Faun.* That country

> ... was chiefly valuable to him as affording a sort of poetic or fairy precinct, where actualities would not be so terribly insisted upon as they are, and needs must be, in America. No author, without a trial, can conceive of the difficulty of writing a romance about a country where there is no shadow, no antiquity, no mystery, no picturesque and gloomy wrong, nor anything but a commonplace prosperity, in broad and simple daylight, as is happily the case with my dear native land.

"Broad and simple daylight" is never enough for Hawthorne, although sunlight is the most important element in his pictorial theory of literature. For the full picture, moonlight, firelight, and darkness are needed as well. As Miriam says in *The Marble Faun*, in art light depends upon shadow.

II. THE SCARLET LETTER

THE SCARLET LET-TER, a tale of sin and concealment, is a dark book, and yet the sun is central to it. With regard to its darkness, let us review some of the evidence. The first scene in the story is laid at "the black flower of civilized society, a prison," which is "marked with weather-stains and other indications of age," giving "a yet darker aspect to its beetle-browed and gloomy front." The rosebush at its threshold has more cheerful implications, but it can only "relieve the darkening close of a tale of human frailty and sorrow." The last sentence of the book describes the heraldic device on the tombstone of Hester Prynne and Arthur Dimmesdale, which "might serve for a motto and brief description of our now concluded legend; so sombre is it, and relieved only by one ever-glowing point of light gloomier than the shadow. . . ."

Throughout the story Dimmesdale, who conceals himself, is pale; he has hidden away from the sun. Chillingworth, his persecutor and fellow victim, grows darker with the story itself. At his first appearance (Chapter III, "The Recognition") Chillingworth's face is seen as "darkened with some powerful emotion." At the end, on the "weather-darkened scaffold," Chillingworth thrusts himself through the crowd, "or, perhaps, so dark, disturbed, and evil" is his look, he has risen from "some nether region," to snatch back his victim from what he intends to do. For Dimmesdale at long last is about to expose himself to the sun, which, "but little past its meridian," shines down upon the clergyman and gives a "distinctness to his figure," making him stand out "from all the earth, to put in his plea of guilty at the bar of Eternal Justice."

One risks tedium, perhaps, by noting in detail the references to sunlight in *The Scarlet Letter*, but the book itself may rescue us through form. It would appear plain matter of fact that "the bright morning sun" shines down on the "broad shoulders and well-developed busts" and the "round and ruddy cheeks" of the matrons of Boston who wait for Hester to be led from prison. Yet the sun is relevant; and the beadle who precedes her is "like a black shadow emerging into sunshine." Pearl, in Hester's arms, blinks and turns away from the "too vivid light of day"; her life until now has acquainted her only with the "gray twilight of a dungeon, or other darksome apartment of the prison." Pearl's introduction to the open light of day is a harsh one.

Hester's beauty and vitality are enhanced by exposure. Her "dark and abundant hair" is so glossy that it throws off the sunshine "with a gleam." Rather than being "dimmed and obscured by a disastrous cloud," her beauty shines out and makes a "halo of the misfortune and ignominy" in which she is enveloped. Her brightness is, however, unnatural; to a sensitive observer, there is "something exquisitely painful in it." She is making a great and defiant effort of will to endure the ordeal prepared for her. " 'Mistress Prynne,' " says the beadle, " 'shall be set where man, woman, and child may have a fair sight of her brave apparel, from this time till an hour past meridian. A blessing on the righteous Colony of the Massachusetts, where iniquity is dragged out into the sunshine!' " When, however, she is suddenly confronted with Chillingworth, the remorseless publicity is almost a relief; a private interview would perhaps have been more terrible than to meet him "with the hot, mid-day sun burning down upon her face, and lighting up its shame."

The two clergymen who now stand forth are in their different ways unacquainted with the sunlight. There is a touch of humor in the account of "the reverend and famous John Wilson." His reaction to the sunshine is like that of the three-month-old Pearl, and he possesses about as much worldly wisdom: "His gray eyes, accustomed to the shaded light of his study," are "winking, like those of Hester's infant, in the unadulterated sunshine." He resembles the "darkly engraved portraits which we see prefixed to old volumes of sermons," and he has "no more right than one of those portraits would have to step forth . . . and meddle with a question of human guilt, passion, and anguish."

The more complex Dimmesdale is first mentioned simply as "a pale young man." More elaborately described:

> . . . there was an air about this young minister,—an apprehensive, a startled, a half-frightened look,—as of a being who felt himself quite astray and at a loss in the pathway of human existence, and could only be at ease in some seclusion

of his own. Therefore, so far as his duties would permit, he trod in the shadowy by-paths, and thus kept himself simple and childlike; coming forth, when occasion was, with a freshness, and fragrance, and dewy purity of thought, which, as many people said, affected them like the speech of an angel.

This passage is of course under the circumstances supremely ironic, like Dimmesdale's own situation, called forth as he is to exhort Hester to reveal her partner in sin—himself. Yet his innocence and freshness are also genuine, and "shadowy by-paths" have their virtues, as Hawthorne attests elsewhere in talking about himself. One may recall here the comparable ambiguity of Hester's halo, and the suggestion that a papist "might have seen in this beautiful woman, so picturesque in her attire and mien, and with the infant at her bosom, an object to remind him of the image of Divine Maternity." The conclusion cannot, however, be ignored that the world is "only the darker for this woman's beauty, and the more lost" for the infant that she has borne.

Hester Prynne's term of confinement is now at an end. Her prison door is thrown open, and she comes forth "into the sunshine, which, falling on all alike," seems, "to her sick and morbid heart, as if meant for no other purpose than to reveal the scarlet letter on her breast." Thus, at the beginning of Chapter V, "Hester at Her Needle," begins Hester's long ordeal of "daily custom," unsupported by the unnatural stimulus of her formal degradation, in which "the combative energy of her character" enables her "to convert the scene into a kind of lurid triumph." She now, in figure at least, passes out of the sun. Not that her ex-

25

posure is relieved, but perhaps that its dreariness makes sunlight inappropriate to it; it now lies in the merciless gaze of the beholders. Her situation is symbolized in the physical situation of her dwelling by the sea:

> A clump of scrubby trees, such as alone grew on the peninsula, did not so much conceal the cottage from view, as seem to denote that here was some object which would fain have been, or at least ought to be concealed.

The light transfers itself to Pearl, like the scarlet letter the mystic symbol of her original sin, whom Hester clothes in scarlet and gold.

"How strange it seemed to the sad woman, as she watched the growth, and the beauty that became every day more brilliant, and the intelligence that threw its quivering sunshine over the tiny features of this child!" Pearl's is the sunlight of truth, of physical vitality, and (I speak advisedly) of the divine innocence of childhood. She has great potentialities for good and also for evil. Hawthorne describes her as "a being whose elements were perhaps beautiful and brilliant, but all in disorder; or with an order peculiar to themselves, amidst which the point of variety and arrangement was difficult or impossible to be discovered." Somewhat later on, Roger Chillingworth is to ask the question, " 'Hath she any discoverable principle of being?' " to be answered by Dimmesdale, " 'None,— save the freedom of a broken law.' "

Within the pattern of sunlight Pearl's case is thus:

> The mother's impassioned state had been the medium through which were transmitted to the unborn infant the rays of its moral life; and, however white and clear ori-

ginally, they had taken the deep stains of crimson and gold, the fiery lustre, the black shadow, and the untempered light of the intervening substance.

In Chapter VIII, "The Elf-Child and the Minister," the Reverend Mr. Wilson makes the same observation in a different context: " 'Methinks I have seen just such figures, when the sun has been shining through a richly painted window, and tracing out the golden and crimson images across the floor." The earlier passage is followed by the statement that Pearl's wild moods (derived from Hester's passion) are now "illuminated by the morning radiance of a young child's disposition, but later in the day of earthly existence might be prolific of the storm and whirlwind."

This original clear white light is genuine; whether it may be permanent is a question at this juncture too difficult to answer. It can be said, however, that Hawthorne's figures are reminiscent of Shelley's lines in *Adonais*:

> *Life, like a dome of many-colored glass*
> *Stains the white radiance of Eternity.*

Further, there is a similar white-light-and-stained-glass parallel to be found in *The Marble Faun*, which appears to locate reality and permanence in the light. The problem is complicated by the reference to "morning radiance," which leads us to Wordsworth's "Ode on Intimations of Immortality from Recollections of Early Childhood," where, as Cleanth Brooks has most clearly shown, morning sunlight is of considerable importance. In the "Ode" the perception of the child is a "celestial light,/The glory and the freshness of a dream," and "the sunshine is a glorious birth." The question for Wordsworth is, of course,

"Whither is fled the visionary gleam," to be partially answered by:

> *... those first affections,*
> *Those shadowy recollections,*
> *Which, be they what they may,*
> *Are yet the fountain light of all our day,*
> *Are yet a master light of all our seeing.*

The "Ode" has its "trailing clouds of glory," "the light, and whence it flows," and its "vision splendid." Perhaps we must also note that

> *At length the man perceives it die away,*
> *And fade into the light of common day,*

since the light of common day certainly is a problem with Hawthorne as well.

Wordsworth, one may think, comes dangerously close to impaling himself on a sharp contradiction between assertion and denial when he concedes

> *What though the radiance which was once so bright*
> *Be now for ever taken from my sight,*
> *Though nothing can bring back the hour*
> *Of splendour in the grass, of glory in the flower. . . .*

(Hawthorne, incidentally, speaks of "the *splendor* of Pearl's own proper beauty," and the word is a favorite with Shelley.) Wordsworth's solution lies, however, in the faith in or construction of continuity itself. No experience, when properly viewed and valued, is ever really lost; it is a vital and harmonious part of the organic unity of the whole. Hawthorne has less confidence in organic unity or synthesis, but "morning radiance" is dear to him in *The Scarlet Letter* and elsewhere. Pearl's morning radiance is real but endangered.

Thus, seen from without, she is rather fire than sunlight, in her costume of crimson and gold. Hers is a beauty that shines "with deep and vivid tints; a bright complexion, eyes possessing intensity both of depth and glow, and hair already of a deep, glossy brown, and which, in after years," will be "nearly akin to black." There is "fire in her and throughout her"; she seems to be "the unpremeditated offshoot of a passionate moment." The description is reminiscent of Hester as she first emerges from the jail, especially in the particular of her glossy, shining hair. Pearl is, indeed, "the very brightest little jet of flame that ever danced upon the earth." And this fire has its darkness, for she is "the scarlet letter in another form; the scarlet letter endowed with life," and the flame is scorching. Hester herself, "as if the red ignominy were so deeply scorched into her brain that all her conceptions assumed its form," has "carefully wrought out the similitude."

Yet Pearl seeks the sunshine. In Chapter VII, "The Governor's Hall," Governor Bellingham's house, new and hopeful, is remarkably sunny, unlike the gloomy Puritan jail. It has "the cheerfulness, gleaming forth from the sunny windows, of a human habitation, into which death had never entered." Its walls are embedded with fragments of broken glass so that, when the sunshine falls "aslant-wise over the front of the edifice," it glitters and sparkles "as if diamonds had been flung against it by the double handful." At the sight of "this bright wonder" Pearl begins to "caper and dance" and demands that "the whole breadth of sunshine should be stripped off its front, and given her to play with." Hester replies to her daughter that she must gather her own sunshine. " 'I have none to give thee!' " This shining house contains the Governor's suit of armor, "so highly burnished as to glow with white radiance, and scatter an illumination everywhere about upon the floor." Pearl is attracted to the gleaming breastplate, a convex mirror in which Hester's scarlet letter is "represented in exaggerated and gigantic proportions, so as to be greatly the most prominent feature of her appearance." The head-piece also produces the reflection of the letter. The child, smiling with "elfish intelligence" and "naughty merriment," particularly calls Hester's attention to this visual effect.

Dimmesdale, the man of shadow and concealment, has been summoned with the Reverend Mr. Wilson to Governor Bellingham's to inquire into Pearl's spiritual state. He is linked with her in Chapter VIII, "The Elf-Child and the Minister." He is, as always, pale, and "his large dark eyes" (at the end of the book to be "those bright dying eyes" as he looks "far into eternity") have "a world of pain in their troubled and melancholy depth." He effectively defends both Hester and the child, but he avoids the light. He stands "with his face partially concealed in the heavy folds of the window-curtains," while the "shadow of his figure," which the sunlight casts upon the floor, is "tremulous with the vehemence of his appeal." Since the subsequent chapters are concerned with the relationship between the gradually declining Dimmesdale and the gradually darkening Roger Chillingworth, they are somber.

In Chapter IX, "The Leech," Dimmesdale now lives with his physician, Chillingworth, in the house of a pious widow, whose "motherly care" has assigned to him "a front apartment, with a sunny exposure, and heavy window-curtains, to create a noontide shadow, when desirable." It might be added that the house has a graveyard beside it and that Dimmesdale's wall tapestries depict the story of "David and Bathsheba, and Nathan the Prophet, in colors still unfaded," but which make the "fair woman of the scene almost as grimly picturesque as the woe-denouncing seer." The minister is not lacking in reminders of sin and death, if he needs any. Chillingworth in turn is slowly becoming darker, like the weatherbeaten jail and the scaffold. Rumor has it that in his Indian captivity he has joined in the incantations of "powerful enchanters," who have performed seemingly miraculous cures by "their skill in the black art." There is "something ugly and evil in his face" not previously present. "According to the vulgar idea, the fire in his laboratory" has been brought "from the lower regions" and is "fed with infernal fuel." Thus, "as might be expected," his face is "getting sooty with the smoke." In Chapter X, "The Leech and His Patient," he has become a "dark miner" working in the soil to uncover "all that dark treasure" of the poor minister's heart (Chapter XI, "The Interior of a Heart"). Later he is to say to Hester, "with gloomy sternness": " 'By thy first step awry thou didst plant the germ of evil; but since that moment, it has all been a dark necessity. . . . Let the black flower blossom as it may!' " In the meantime, Hester avoids the light also (Chapter XIII, "Another View of Hester"), from a motive that might be pride, but was so like humility, that it produced all the softening influence of the latter quality on the public mind. . . . It was only the darkened house that could contain her. When sunshine came again, she was not there. Her shadow had faded across the threshold.

Also, she has either cut off or concealed her luxuriant hair, so that "not a shining lock of it ever once" escapes into the sunshine.

In the darkness of his heart Dimmesdale wanders amid fantasies:

It is the unspeakable misery of a life so false as his, that it steals the pith and substance out of whatever realities there are around us, and which were meant by Heaven to be the spirit's joy and nutriment. To the untrue man, the whole universe is false,—it is impalpable,—it shrinks to nothing within his grasp. And he himself, in so far as he shows himself in a false light, becomes a shadow, or, indeed, ceases to exist.

Seeking some measure of peace, he decides to expose himself, as Hester has been exposed, upon the scaffold (Chapter XII, "The Minister's Vigil"). "Walking in the shadow of a dream," however, he does alone and at night, in obscurity and unreality:

If the same multitude which had stood as eye-witnesses while Hester Prynne sustained her punishment could now have been summoned forth, they would have discerned no face above the platform, nor hardly the outline of a human shape, in the dark gray of the midnight. But the town was all asleep. There was no peril of discovery.

Amid this darkness the minister nevertheless is "overcome with a great horror of mind, as if the universe were gazing at a scarlet token on his naked breast, right over his heart." He shrieks aloud, and at the sound a lamp is lit in Governor Bellingham's mansion. The old governor himself looks out, and to another window comes Mistress Hibbins, his witchlike sister. They see nothing, however, and their lamps are extinguished.

Another light appears, that of the Reverend Mr. Wilson, who is making his way homeward "from the death-chamber of Governor Winthrop," who has "passed from earth to heaven within that very hour." Mr. Wilson's lantern surrounds him "with a radiant halo" that glorifies him "amid this gloomy night of sin,—as if the departed Governor had left him an inheritance of his glory, or as if he had caught upon himself the distant shine of the celestial city. . . ." He passes on, and Hester and Pearl appear from the same deathbed, and are summoned by the minister to stand with him on the scaffold. The three form "an electric chain," as they stand hand in hand. Pearl, creature of the sun, asks persistently, " 'Wilt thou stand here with mother and me, to-morrow noontide?' " to be answered by Dimmesdale, " 'At the great judgment day. . . . But the daylight of this world shall not see our meeting!' "

But now they are irradiated in a light which might well be of judgment day itself, portentous, prophetic—the light of a meteor:

> The great vault brightened, like the dome of an immense lamp. It showed the familiar scene of the street, with the distinctness of mid-day, but also with the awfulness that is always imparted to familiar objects by an unaccustomed light. The wooden houses, with their jutting stories and quaint gable-peaks; the doorsteps and thresholds, with the

early grass springing up about them; the garden-plots, black with freshly-turned earth; the wheel-track, little worn, and, even in the market-place, margined with green on either side,—all were visible, but with a singularity of aspect that seemed to give another moral interpretation to the things of this world than they had ever borne before. And there stood the minister, with his hand over his heart; and Hester Prynne, with the embroidered letter glimmering on her bosom; and little Pearl, herself a symbol, and the connecting link between those two. They stood in the noon of that strange and solemn splendor, as if it were the light that is to reveal all secrets, and the daybreak that shall unite all who belong to one another.

The passage is of great importance. In the first place, it is a notation of Hawthorne's degree of reliance upon the Romantic imagination, which sees ordinary and familiar things in an unusual light. This light *is* reliable, "with the *distinctness* of mid-day," an attribute which belongs to the high Romantic formula for the picturesque, but which is also in Hawthorne a sign of reality. It is genuinely prophetic, a "*noon* of that strange and solemn splendor, as if it were the light that is to reveal all secrets." It is nevertheless not all-sufficient; the meteor itself suggests both transience and possible deceit. It is not durable, and Hawthorne values more greatly than do Coleridge and Wordsworth the quality of usualness in itself. The light is associated with the morbid and obsessive state of the minister's mind, emphasized in his interpretation of the immense *A* that he presently sees in the sky:

But what shall we say, when an individual discovers a revelation addressed to himself alone!   We impute it, therefore, solely to the disease in his own eye and heart, that the minister, looking upward to the zenith, beheld there the appearance of an immense letter,—the letter A,—marked out in lines of dull red light.

This skepticism is doubtless in part an ambiguity, to soften the effect for artistic purposes of Hawthorne's otherwise too-explicit symbol; also, it cannot be completely subjective without destroying the interest of the problem itself. One concludes that this light, as has been said, represents an important, but not the total, truth. It is a part, an element, not the whole.

In the crucial forest chapters of *The Scarlet Letter* (Chapters XVI to XIX), Hester Prynne, like Dimmesdale, also wanders in the darkness of the heart. She asks herself, "in bitterness of heart," whether Pearl should have been born at all. "Indeed, the same dark question" often comes into her mind, "with reference to the whole race of womanhood. . . . Thus, Hester Prynne," whose heart has "lost its regular and healthy throb," wanders "without a clew in the dark labyrinth of mind." There is "wild and ghastly scenery all around her, and a home and comfort nowhere." In this, her darkest hour, she determines that Dimmesdale must be made aware of the identity of Chillingworth, the source of the evil that surrounds the minister. Her only excuse for the concealment has been that she has been able to discern "no method of rescuing him from a blacker ruin" than has "overwhelmed herself, except by acquiescing in Roger Chillingworth's scheme of disguise." When she encounters the physician, she sees that Chillingworth himself has deteriorated greatly in the seven years since their last confrontation. Though he tries to disguise himself in the light of a smile, it plays him false and flickers over his face "so derisively" that the spectator can "see his blackness all the better for it." In their interview Hester begs him to forgive the minister, as the only escape " ' for him, or thee, or me, who are here wandering together in this gloomy maze of evil.' " But Chillingworth refuses and creeps away, a dark specter, banished from the sun:

> Did the sun, which shone so brightly everywhere else, really fall upon him? Or was there, as it rather seemed, a circle of ominous shadow moving along with his deformity, whichever way he turned himself? . . . Or would he spread bat's wings and flee away, looking so much the uglier the higher he rose towards heaven?

As Hester looks after him, "The emotions of that brief space" throw a "dark light" on her state of mind, "revealing much that she might not otherwise have acknowledged to herself."

Few readers of *The Scarlet Letter* can have failed to notice Hawthorne's use of sunlight in the forest scenes. A detailed re-examination of the sun images in these chapters revealed a striking emphasis upon Pearl that I had not perceived in earlier readings. The sun persistently follows her and shines only fleetingly upon Hester and the minister. Rereading has also emphasized the central importance to the book of the meeting in the forest. Hester, discerning how close both she and Dimmesdale are to spiritual collapse, has made her decision to move toward the light by informing the minister of his true situation, exposed to the eye of his enemy, Chillingworth. Determined to clear the air, she has announced her purpose to Chilling-worth himself. In one significant respect, however, she has failed in candor. To Pearl's direct and deadly questions: " 'Mother, . . . what does the scarlet letter mean?' " and " 'Mother!—Mother!—Why does the minister keep his hand over his heart?' " Hester cannot bring herself to reply. " 'Do not tease me,' " she says angrily, " 'else I shall shut thee into the dark closet!' "

With matters thus, in Chapter XVI, "A Forest Walk," Hester and Pearl move along a straggling footpath "on-ward into the mystery of the primeval forest," which hems it in "so narrowly" and stands "so black and dense on either side" and discloses "such imperfect glimpses of the sky above" that, to Hester's mind, it symbolizes the "moral wilderness" in which she has "so long been wandering." It is a gray day, but with "a gleam of flickering sunshine," a "flitting cheerfulness" that is "always at the farther ex-tremity of some long vista through the forest." The sun-light withdraws itself as they come near and leaves the spots where it has danced "the drearier," because they have "hoped to find them bright." Pearl, whom, as we have seen, her mother has just failed, challenges Hester directly:

" 'Mother, . . . the sunshine does not love you. It runs away and hides itself, because it is afraid of something on your bosom. . . . Stand you here, and let me run and catch it. I am but a child. It will not flee from me, for I wear nothing on my bosom yet!' " Pearl does "catch the sun-shine" and stands "laughing in the midst of it, all bright-ened by its splendor, and scintillating with the vivacity excited by rapid motion." Hester, however, is denied the

37

light, which as she approaches is re-absorbed into Pearl.
As Hester tries to grasp it,

> the sunshine vanished; or, to judge from the bright expres-
> sion that was dancing on Pearl's features, her mother could
> have fancied that the child had absorbed it into herself, and
> would give it forth again, with a gleam about her path, as
> they should plunge into some gloomier shade.

Yet Pearl's vivacity is "a doubtful charm, imparting a
hard, metallic lustre to the child's character." And she asks
Hester to tell her a story about the Black Man who haunts
the forest.

For some time the only light in the forest is the reflection
from a little brook, Pearl's counterpart, though "unlike
the little stream," Pearl dances and sparkles, and prattles
"airily along her course." Pearl now wanders away for a
little distance, and Dimmesdale appears. Within the dark
forest and wrapped in his own darkness, he does not know
whether Hester is "a woman or a shadow." In the crucial
interview that follows, the two attempt to find their way
back to one another. Dimmesdale avows the spiritual
agony of his deception and self-concealment, that he
must " 'stand up in my pulpit, and meet so many eyes
turned upward to my face, as if the light of heaven were
beaming from it! . . . and then look inward, and discern
the black reality of what they idolize?' " At long last
Hester reveals to him that his physician, Chillingworth, is
her husband; a revelation greeted by the minister

> with all that violence of passion, which . . . was, in fact, the
> portion of him which the Devil claimed, and through which
> he sought to win the rest. Never was there a blacker or a

38

fiercer frown than Hester now encountered. For the brief space that it lasted, it was a dark transfiguration.

At length reconciled, they sit down together, hand in hand.

Life had never brought them a gloomier hour; it was the point whither their pathway had so long been tending, and darkening ever, as it stole along; and yet it enclosed a charm that made them linger upon it . . . . No golden light had ever been so precious as the gloom of this dark forest. . . .

It is a momentary refuge from prying eyes and reprehension. Persuaded by Hester to escape with her (Chapter XVIII), Dimmesdale gazes into Hester's face "with a look in which hope and joy shone out, indeed, but with fear betwixt them, and a kind of horror at her boldness . . . ." The decision made, ". . . a glow of strange enjoyment" throws "its flickering brightness over the trouble of his breast." Hester now ritually discards the scarlet letter and frees her hair from the cap that confines it:

. . . down it fell upon her shoulders, dark and rich, with at once a shadow and a light in its abundance, and imparting the charm of softness to her features. There played around her mouth, and beamed out of her eyes, a radiant and tender smile, that seemed gushing from the very heart of womanhood. A crimson flush was glowing on her cheek, that had been long so pale.

Now,

. . . as if the gloom of the earth and sky had been lent the effluence of these two mortal hearts, it vanished with their sorrow. All at once, as with a sudden smile of heaven, forth

burst the sunshine, pouring a very flood into the obscure
forest, gladdening each green leaf, transmuting the yellow
fallen ones to gold, and gleaming adown the gray trunks of
the solemn trees. The objects that had made a shadow hitherto, embodied the brightness now. The course of the little
brook might be traced by its merry gleam afar into the
wood's heart of mystery, which had become a mystery
of joy.

All, indeed, is transfigured; and one remarks as well that
in Hawthorne distinctness itself as well as embodiment
are virtues, since they denote reality. The scene is an
epiphany—and yet we quickly find that there are other
considerations to deal with, and another kind of light.

For this is the light of Nature, that same Nature whose
deep heart in the rosebush before the prison door could
pity and show kindness to the condemned criminal:

> ... the sympathy of Nature—that wild, heathen Nature of
> the forest, never subjugated by human law, nor illumined
> by higher truth—with the bliss of these two spirits! Love,
> whether newly born, or aroused from a death-like slumber,
> must always create a sunshine, filling the heart so full of
> radiance, that it overflows upon the outward world.

Nature is real and indispensable, and the Puritans have
sorely erred in expelling her with a fork, for she always
comes rushing back. She is not all-sufficient, however, as
the two lovers quickly discover with the return of Pearl,
whom they first glimpse

> in a streak of sunshine, a good way off, on the other side of
> the brook, ... like a bright-apparelled vision, in a sunbeam,
> which fell down upon her through an arch of boughs. The

ray quivered to and fro, making her figure dim or distinct,— now like a real child, now like a child's spirit,—as the splendor went and came again.

The ambiguity of this light presents the problem, as Pearl's figure becomes alternately dim and distinct. On the one hand, it expresses the real divinity and sanctity of childhood, "trailing clouds of glory" ("like a child's spirit"), but it is dangerously fugitive as well. Pearl, like Blake's Thel, is between two worlds, and she cannot remain so. She must be embodied; she must be found or else lost irretrievably. As a symbol of the letter, too, she fights for her significance. She, too, has been immersed in Nature, in the hour "while her mother sat talking with the clergyman," for "the great black forest—stern as it showed itself to those who brought the guilt and troubles of the world into its bosom—became the playmate of the lonely infant, as well as it knew how." It offers her berries, the woodland beasts have no fear of her, and even "a wolf, it is said,—but here the tale has surely lapsed into the improbable,—came up, and smelt of Pearl's robe, and offered his savage head to be patted by her hand." Yet however endearing this sympathy may be, it is no firm base for a human being, as later with the primitive Donatello in *The Marble Faun*. "The truth seems to be, however, that the mother-forest, and these wild things which it nourished, all recognized a kindred wildness in the human child."

As has already been suggested, the light upon Pearl also reflects her uncertain and dangerous state, with heaven on one side and extinction on the other. She is beautiful and yet hauntingly elusive. A pool reflects "a perfect image of her little figure, with all the brilliant picturesqueness of her beauty, in its adornment of flowers and wreathed foliage, but more refined and spiritualized than the reality." This is Hawthorne's symbol of perfect art, as his "Old Manse" essay will attest, but in this instance its doubleness denotes dubiety. "This image, so nearly identical with the living Pearl," seems to "communicate somewhat of its own shadowy and intangible quality to the child herself."

The impression is enforced from the point of view of Hester and Dimmesdale:

> It was strange, the way in which Pearl stood, looking so steadfastly at them through the dim medium of the forest-gloom; herself, meanwhile, all glorified with a ray of sunshine that was attracted thitherward as by a certain sympathy. In the brook beneath stood another child,—another and the same,—with likewise its ray of golden light. Hester felt herself, in some indistinct and tantalizing manner, estranged from Pearl.

The light and the truth are with Pearl, unbeknownst to herself. For her sake they must be correctly interpreted, and Hester fails in understanding. There are "both truth and error in the impression"; the child and mother are "estranged, but through Hester's fault, not Pearl's." The sunlight remains with the child as with inexorable determination she forces Hester to take up the scarlet letter once more:

> At length, assuming a singular air of authority, Pearl stretched out her hand, with the small forefinger extended, and pointing evidently towards her mother's breast. And beneath, in the mirror of the brook, there was the flower-girdled and sunny image of little Pearl, pointing her small forefinger too.

Hester's own sunlight is taken from her by the more powerful light that accompanies her child, as she reaffixes the letter and once more hides her rich and shining hair beneath her cap. As if there is "a withering spell in the sad letter, her beauty, the warmth and richness of her womanhood," departs, "like fading sunshine," and "a gray shadow" seems to "fall across her." The forest scene ends, and the shadow foretells the remainder of *The Scarlet Letter*.

Leaving the forest and Hester, Dimmesdale finds that he has undergone a fundamental change. In Chapter XX, "The Minister in a Maze," he looks forth with a doubleness of vision that reminds us of the ambiguities of the bright but elusive Pearl. Returning to his Election Sermon, left unfinished two days before, he seems "to stand apart, and eye" the man who has written it

> with scornful, pitying, but half-envious curiosity. That self was gone. Another man had returned out of the forest; a wiser one; with a knowledge of hidden mysteries which the simplicity of the former never could have reached. A bitter kind of knowledge that!

Dimmesdale's whole state of mind, and along with it the purport of the great Election Sermon itself, remain unrevealed to us in any explicit terms until the final moment of decision. He throws away what he has written before the experience of the forest and recommences the sermon as a new man. What is said about its creation is perhaps as close as we come to Dimmesdale's own conclusions:

> . . . he wrote with such an impulsive flow of thought and emotion, that he fancied himself inspired; and only wondered that Heaven should see fit to transmit the grand and

solemn music of its oracles through so foul an organ-pipe as he. However, leaving that mystery to solve itself, or go unsolved forever, he drove his task onward, with earnest haste and ecstasy.

The minister has achieved a pitch of insight impossible without the aberrations and enfranchisements that the forest and Hester have brought him. What he has learned, however, is mystery itself, which must "solve itself, or go unsolved forever." He has accepted his own limitations, and the dualism of the human condition. The inspiration of the Election Sermon is authentic, and it is as it were validated by the sunrise, which throws "a golden beam into the study" and lays it "right across the minister's bedazzled eyes." But the truth of the sermon as it has been conceived and written is not the whole truth of reality or of Dimmesdale himself. As we find, there are to be considered not only its words but the music as well, in the elucidation of its full meaning.

On the climactic day (Chapter XXI, "The New England Holiday") Hester is "clad in a garment of coarse gray cloth," but Pearl is "decked out with airy gayety." The contrast is marked:

> It would have been impossible to guess that this bright and sunny apparition owed its existence to the shape of gloomy gray. . . . The dress, so proper was it to little Pearl, seemed an effluence, or inevitable development and outward manifestation of her character, no more to be separated from her than the many-hued brilliancy from a butterfly's wing, or the painted glory from the leaf of a bright flower.

In addition, there is "a certain singular inquietude and excitement in her mood, resembling nothing so much as the shimmer of a diamond, that sparkles and flashes with the varied throbbings of the breast on which it is displayed." Pearl expresses the emotions that are concealed "in the marble passiveness of Hester's brow," and certainly the light remains principally with her. Thus situated, she points to the close, remarking of Dimmesdale that " 'in the dark night-time he calls us to him, and holds thy hand and mind' " but that " 'here, in the sunny day, and among all the people, he knows us not.' " In Chapter XXII, "The Procession," the witchlike Mistress Hibbins re-emphasizes the point:

> "I know thee, Hester; for I behold the token. We may all see it in the sunshine. . . . But this minister! Let me tell thee, in thine ear! When the Black Man sees one of his own servants, signed and sealed, so shy of owning to the bond as is the Reverend Mr. Dimmesdale, he hath a way of ordering matters so that the mark shall be disclosed in open daylight to the eyes of all the world!"

In the delivery of the great sermon Dimmesdale's secret is darkly revealed, for, "majestic" as his voice sometimes becomes, there is "forever in it an essential character of plaintiveness." However high the minister's purport and voice, the attentive listener can detect "the same cry of pain." It is "this profound and continual undertone" that gives the clergyman "his most appropriate power." The dualism is strong and consummately ironic, but one feels that Dimmesdale has taken account of the irony and conquered the dualism by understanding it at last, so that one effect is reinforced, not canceled, by the other. To his audience,

. . . never had man spoken in so wise, so high, and so holy a spirit, as he that spake this day; nor had inspiration ever breathed through mortal lips more evidently than it did through his.

In "a spirit as of prophecy" the minister has foretold of the New England colonies "a high and glorious destiny for the newly gathered people of the Lord."

The sermon's undertone has not gone unnoticed, but his hearers attribute it to Dimmesdale's physical weakness and

foreboding of untimely death. . . . This idea of his transitory stay on earth gave the last emphasis to the effect which the preacher had produced; it was as if an angel, in his passage to the skies, had shaken his bright wings over the people for an instant,—at once a shadow and a splendor,— and had shed down a shower of golden truths upon them.

The minister totters, exhausted by his great effort and visibly upon the point of death, but refusing support from his companions.

The crowd, meanwhile, looked on with awe and wonder. This earthly faintness was, in their view, only another phase of the minister's celestial strength; nor would it have seemed a miracle too high to be wrought for one so holy, had he ascended before their eyes, waxing dimmer and brighter, and fading at last into the light of heaven.

Once again the situation is at once supremely ironic and yet at the same time genuine. The holiness and the light are authentic, but like Pearl's divinity in the forest, trailing clouds of glory, they are fugitive and provisional; they may instantly vanish or be transformed into darkness.

Indeed, as the minister at last summons Hester and Pearl to his side, the dark principle interposes itself to endeavor a final deception:

> At this instant, old Roger Chillingworth thrust himself through the crowd,—or, perhaps, so dark, disturbed, and evil, was his look, he rose up out of some nether region,— to snatch back his victim from what he sought to do! . . . "Do not blacken your fame, and perish in dishonor!"

But the minister goes on into light and reality, the same light that earlier beat down upon Hester in her exposure to the Puritan crowd—the same crowd—and on the same scaffold:

> The sun, but little past its meridian, shone down upon the clergyman, and gave a distinctness to his figure, as he stood out from all the earth, to put in his plea of guilty at the bar of Eternal Justice.

As was affirmed at the outset, *The Scarlet Letter* is a gloomy book, despite the visitations of the sun. The "ever-glowing point of light" of its conclusion is said to be "gloomier than the shadow." Justice having been meted out to Dimmesdale—and Hester—at the bar of Eternal Justice, they are left to its mercy in another sphere. But Pearl, the child of their sin, is redeemed. In her the sun triumphs, and it is hoped that this investigation of the light imagery that surrounds her is of use in demonstrating the artistic logic of her final emergence into light.

III. THE HOUSE OF THE SEVEN GABLES

HAWTHORNE'S characters should never be studied in isolation. They are basically symbolic, and out of context they appear incomplete and unsatisfactory. Hawthorne's view of life does not permit of the dominant hero or heroine, nor does he encourage us to identify ourselves with his brain children as individuals. In all his major novels his principal characters come in groups; in *The House of the Seven Gables* there are Phoebe, Judge Pyncheon, Hepzibah, Clifford, and Holgrave. Phoebe is the agent of good in the story, as the Judge is the agent of evil. Hepzibah and Clifford Pyncheon have been overshadowed by the eclipsing curse of the House, so that they are powerless to help themselves. The Judge attacks them, and Phoebe's influence saves them. Holgrave, who has least to do with the action, hovers as it were between audience and stage. Hepzibah and Clifford, the most interesting of the dramatis personae, are passive. More complex and profound than the youthful Phoebe, they are nevertheless helpless without her.

All these characters are incomplete in themselves.

Phoebe is too sweet, a mere ingénue; Hepzibah and Clifford are a bit ludicrous, and in their defenselessness nearly contemptible; the Judge is too melodramatically villainous; and Holgrave too lightly and dryly drawn. Yet together they make up a design, and it is incorrect to suppose that Hawthorne intended them to be other than they are. While he did not believe that individuals can wholly control their destinies or achieve an ideally full development, he nevertheless attached great importance to the individual as symbol, as actor in a mystery drama of good and evil. Let us examine, then, the relation of the characters of *The House of the Seven Gables* to a part of Hawthorne's world of symbol, a place of light and darkness and of various shades between.

Despite the "power of blackness" that Melville admired in Hawthorne, his world has its solar system. The sun is its center, the divine light and the source of light. Sunlight also represents reality, on different levels, but perhaps ideally on some occasions merging. These levels range between the extremes of the literal and the imaginative. The sunlight of imagination is the slanting ray of early morning or late afternoon, like the "accidents of sunset and moonlight" of Coleridge's "poetry of nature," in which ordinary landscapes become transfigured. The literal sunlight belongs to the broad noon of common day. In his use of the sun as a symbol of God, Hawthorne is following the traditional Judaeo-Christian way. His employment of the slanting ray, however, is a Romantic rejection of literalism, or at least a new light cast upon it.

As the story of the Pyncheons, *The House of the Seven Gables* has a dominant sunshine-storm, or light-darkness, pattern, originating in the physical properties of the house itself. "The aspect of the venerable mansion," says the narrator, "has always affected me like a human countenance, bearing the traces not merely of outward storm and sunshine, but expressive also of the long lapse of mortal life, and accompanying vicissitudes, that have passed within." Thus sunshine and storm are both literally and symbolically the weathering of two hundred years of varied fortunes. In this application, sunshine stands for general good fortune, for material prosperity, and for harmonious kinship with society. Storm and darkness are correspondingly misfortune and the isolation of the original Pyncheon sin, which Phoebe, free of its curse, successfully relieves by her light.

Phoebe is doubtless too obviously "our little ray of sunshine," but we shall find that her accompanying imagery is solid, consistent, and fully imagined. Behind her stands a complex of symbols that is present in all of Hawthorne's fiction. She is a sun goddess, of dawn, of spring and early summer, delicately tanned, though never fully exposed— on one occasion we find her using a sunshade. The final secret of Hawthorne's values, at any rate in *The House of the Seven Gables*, is moderation, which is in consequence the key to his characters. It is remarked of Phoebe, weeping with shock at Clifford's attempt to throw himself from the window (Chapter XI, "The Arched Window"), that all extravagance is a horror to her. Thus she is spring sunshine, dawn light, a golden mean.

Phoebe's sunshine must be supplemented by another kind of light. Typically in Hawthorne, no single character, attribute, or gift is all-sufficient. In *The Scarlet*

Letter, as we have seen, the lurid portent of the meteor has a genuine if special validity. So in the Pyncheon garden, at the moment when Phoebe and Holgrave fall in love, the insight of the clear sun is enriched by the subtler, more romantic shading of moonlight. This moonlight deepens Phoebe's perceptions, as well as the perceptions of the rational-minded Holgrave. It represents the essential truth provided by art and illuminates Hawthorne's distinction between the romance and the novel. "The former," he says, in the Preface to *The House of the Seven Gables*,

> while, as a work of art, it must rigidly subject itself to laws, and while it sins unpardonably, so far as it may swerve aside from the truth of the human heart—has fairly a right to present that truth under circumstances, to a great extent, of the writer's own choosing or creation. If he thinks fit, also, he may so manage his atmospherical medium as to bring out or mellow the lights and deepen and enrich the shadows of the picture.

Thus he adds moonlight to sunshine, as the sunny Phoebe is herself educated by contact with this other medium.

A preliminary word about other characters. Clifford Pyncheon is originally pure aesthete and hedonist, a butterfly of the sun. His long years in prison, however, have alienated him from light. His basic image is a thin gray cloud, through which rays of sunlight sporadically break. In keeping with his broken, aimless life, Clifford is dim and indeterminate of outline. When Phoebe first encounters him (Chapter VI, "Maule's Well"), she cannot see him; she has only a sense of some living presence and inquires of Hepzibah, " 'Is there not some one in the room with us?' "

Hepzibah and Judge Pyncheon are mirror images of each other, for she is dark without and he within. His sunshine is all on the surface. Poor Hepzibah's dark scowl, the counterpart of the dark-browed house itself, is both the cause and the effect of her isolation from society. It is a tragic irony that her heart is soft and loving, while outwardly genial Judge is hard as a rock. Indeed, Hawthorne's image of the Judge's inward self is alternately a gray adamantine rock and a heavily brooding cloud, endued with a coldness that is the precise opposite of his outward warmth.

The judge is a false sun god; his benevolence is counterfeit. His evil is manifested in excess and discordance, in contrast to the harmony of Phoebe. He passes from one extreme to the other. Drawing back instinctively from the Judge's cousinly kiss (Chapter VIII, "The Pyncheon of Today"), Phoebe is startled by the sudden change in his face:

> It was quite as striking, allowing for the difference of scale, as that betwixt a landscape under a broad sunshine, and just before a thunderstorm; not that it had the passionate intensity of the latter aspect, but was cold, hard, immitigable, like a day-long brooding cloud.

A little later the Judge beams upon Hepzibah "with a smile, so broad and sultry, that, had it been only half as warm as it looked, a trellis of grapes might at once have turned purple under its summer-like exposure."

There is a certain balance in the storm and sunshine, the light and the darkness which have constituted the history of the house of the seven gables, and with it a certain suggestion that its humanity and its dignity are inseparable from its vicissitudes. Perhaps the darkness is prevalent, as "the venerable mansion . . . grew black in the prevalent east-wind," but, as in his reflections on the city of Rome in *The Marble Faun*, Hawthorne's attitude is ambivalent. The darkness is early foreshadowed: "The terror and ugliness of Maule's crime, and the wretchedness of his punishment, would darken the freshly plastered walls, and infect them early with the scent of an old and melancholy house." Yet this quality is inseparable from its human warmth of meaning: "as the scene of events more full of human interest, perhaps, than those of a gray, feudal castle —familiar as it stands, in its rusty old-age, it is therefore only the more difficult to imagine the bright novelty with which it first caught the sunshine."

In its beginnings it was as bright as Governor Bellingham's mansion, which so bedazzled Pearl, with "glittering plaster, composed of lime, pebbles, and bits of glass," and "many lattices, with their small, diamond-shaped panes," which "admitted the sunlight into hall and chamber." Yet even here the brightness was qualified. The projecting upper stories cast a "shadow and thoughtful gloom into the lower rooms," and on the newly placed sundial "the sun was still marking the passage of the first bright hour in a history, that was not destined to be all so bright." Darkness, in fact, penetrates the house very soon indeed, in Colonel Pyncheon, wearing in death "a frown on his dark and massive countenance." We remember the wooden prison of *The Scarlet Letter*, prematurely "marked with weather-stains and other indications of age," which give a "yet darker aspect to its beetle-browed and gloomy front," and the association of this place of crime with the cemetery, the abode of death.

The Colonel's death is coupled with the mysterious disappearance of the Pyncheon charter to "the eastern lands" and the subsequent obsession of his descendants with their claims to this vast territory, in "an absurd delusion of family importance." Here again the consequences are both bright and dark;

> In the better specimens of the breed, this peculiarity threw an ideal grace over the hard material of human life, without stealing away any truly valuable quality. In the baser sort, its effect was to increase the liability to sluggishness and dependence, and induce the victim of a shadowy hope to remit all self-effort, while awaiting the realization of his dreams.

Through these subsequent generations the picture of the Colonel broods over the house, its features seeming "so darkly to mingle the shadow of their presence with the sunshine of the passing hour, that no good thoughts or purposes could ever spring up and blossom there." Long after, when the Colonel's successor steps forth to rehabilitate the family, there are few of the Pyncheons left "to sun themselves in the glow of the Judge's prosperity." Meanwhile, the unlucky descendants of Matthew Maule, long immersed in obscurity and darkness, seem to have disappeared for good. But there is a tradition that these night people had exercised a strange ascendancy over their Pyncheon oppressors, in the world of dreams. "The Pyncheons, if all stories were true, haughtily as they bore themselves in the noonday streets of their native town, were no better than bond-servants to these plebeian

Maules, on entering the topsy-turvy commonwealth of sleep."

The narrative proper (Chapter III, "The First Customer") commences with poor Hepzibah, praying at dawn on the day that she must perform the dreadful task of opening her shop for the first time:

> Evidently, this is to be a day of more than ordinary trial to Miss Hepzibah, who, for above a quarter of a century gone-by, has dwelt in strict seclusion; taking no part in the business of life, and just as little in its intercourse and pleasures. Not with such fervor prays the torpid recluse, looking forward to the cold, sunless, stagnant calm of a day that is to be like innumerable yesterdays!

The very crossing of the threshold of her own bedroom door is a crucial moment, a daring act. "Forth she steps into the dusky, time-darkened passage; a tall figure, clad in black silk . . . feeling her way towards the stairs like a near-sighted person, as in truth she is." Shut away from the sun, her blackness, her scowl, have been imposed upon her, an innocent victim. But her heart never frowns. It is "naturally tender, sensitive, and full of little tremors and palpitations," all of which "weaknesses" it retains, while her face is growing "so perversely stern, and even fierce." It is a sad irony that sinner and sinned-against are indistinguishable in their consequences. This scowl, this sternness, this blackness belonged also to the Colonel, the original Pyncheon, as they do to the Judge, the present Pyncheon, though the Judge takes care to conceal these ominous indications of his nature. As Hepzibah passes into the shop to arrange her wares for the first time, "in the aspect of this dark-arrayed, pale-faced, ladylike old figure," there is a "deeply tragic character" that contrasts "irreconcilably with the ludicrous pettiness of her employment."

Hepzibah now has to face the sunlight of everyday reality, which "might now be seen stealing down the front of the opposite house, from the windows of which came a reflected gleam, struggling through the boughs of the elm-tree, and enlightening the interior of the shop, more distinctly than heretofore." At the first ring of the shop bell she rises, "as pale as a ghost at cock-crow"; however, it is not a customer but her lodger, Holgrave. Entering from "the morning light," he appears to bring "some of its cheery influences into the shop along with him." Holgrave is not without his ambiguities, for he has a "dark, high-featured countenance," and a little later "a strange gleam of half-hidden sarcasm" can be observed "flashing through the kindliness of his manner." A daguerreotypist, he remarks that " 'I misuse Heaven's blessed sunshine, by tracing out human features, through its agency.' " Left to herself, poor Hepzibah reflects upon the darkness of her prospects, with her pitiful little shop pitted against "the great thoroughfare of a city, all astir with customers," and its great stores, with "noble mirrors at the farther end of each establishment, doubling all this wealth by a brightly burnished vista of unrealities!" For her part, there is only "the dusky old House of the Seven Gables, with the antiquated shop-window under its projecting story, and Hepzibah herself, in a gown of rusty black silk, behind the counter, scowling at the world" as it goes by. "The house might just as well be buried in an eternal fog," while all other houses have "the sunshine on them."

In her extremity Hepzibah takes courage; indeed, "the healthiest glow" that Hepzibah has known for years has come now, "in the dreaded crisis," when, for the first time, she has "put forth her hand to help herself." The effect, however, is transient; "the despondency of her whole life" threatens to return. It is "like the heavy mass of clouds, which we may often see obscuring the sky, and making a gray twilight everywhere, until, towards nightfall, it yields temporarily to a glimpse of sunshine. But, always, the envious cloud strives to gather again across the streak of celestial azure."

"Towards noon" of this day of ordeal (Chapter IV, "A Day Behind the Counter") Judge Pyncheon appears, wiping perspiration from his brow—a false sun before the advent of the true sunlight of Phoebe. He exudes respectability and benevolence, but he carries with him a private darkness (his gold-headed cane is "a serviceable staff, of dark, polished wood"), along with his public brightness. He is capable of frown and smile alike, and the smile that is "acrid and disagreeable" is charged with "the sunniest complacency and benevolence" when he becomes aware of Hepzibah in her shopwindow. He passes on, leaving Hepzibah with the sudden perception of his resemblance to the ancient portrait of the Colonel, the original Pyncheon. This picture has "almost faded into the canvas, and hidden itself behind the duskiness of age," but "while the physical outline and substance" are "darkening away from the beholder's eye, the bold, hard, and, at the same time, indirect character of the man" seems to be brought out "in a kind of spiritual relief." Put him in the Colonel's clothes, reflects Hepzibah, and " 'then let Jaffrey smile as he might—nobody would doubt that it was the old Pyncheon come again!' " This fancy, however, is treated as a mere product of her loneliness and isolation: She needs a walk "along the noonday street, to keep her sane."

During the course of the same long day, the well-meant encouragement of the old handyman, Uncle Venner, causes Hepzibah to take refuge in fantasies of Pyncheon grandeur. His words kindled "a strange festal glory in the poor, bare, melancholy chambers of her brain, as if that inner world were suddenly lighted up with gas." His "final" and "all-important" advice, however, calls for attributes within her that she does not have. " 'Put on a bright face for your customers, and smile pleasantly as you hand them what they ask for! A stale article, if you dip it in a good, warm, sunny smile, will go off better than a fresh one that you've scowled upon!' " To this, "poor Hepzibah responded with a sigh, so deep and heavy that it almost rustled Uncle Venner quite away."

Help is near, however. On the same evening Hepzibah awaits the arrival of Clifford, released from prison after many years. "Remote and dusky, and with no sunshine on all the intervening space, was that region of the Past, whence her only guest might be expected to arrive! Was she to meet him now?" But it is a young girl who is handed down from the omnibus that stops outside the door of the house—a girl who rewards her "cavalier with a smile, the cheery glow of which" is seen "reflected on his own face" as he re-enters the vehicle. Phoebe, "so fresh, so unconventional, and yet so orderly and obedient to common rules," is "widely in contrast, at that moment, with everything about her." Yet she is somehow immediately at home:

> But—even as a ray of sunshine, fall into what dismal place it may, instantaneously creates for itself a propriety in being there—so did it seem altogether fit that the girl should be standing at the threshold. It was no less evidently proper, that the door should swing open to admit her.

Phoebe Pyncheon awakes the next morning (Chapter V, "May and November") in a chamber that fronts "towards the east; so that, at a very seasonable hour, a glow of crimson light" comes "flooding through the window" to bathe the "dingy ceiling and paper-hangings in its own hue." She is shut in by "a dark, antique canopy" which broods over the girl "like a cloud." But the morning sun soon invades her dark surroundings, with "the caress which a dewy maiden—such as the Dawn is, immortally—gives to her sleeping sister. . . ." Phoebe's endowments are sunlike: she has "the gift of practical arrangement . . . a kind of natural magic, that enables these favored ones to bring out the hidden capabilities of things around them." Her presence at once transforms the house's traditional darkness, like the dawn light itself.

She has a "homely witchcraft" which can reclaim her "waste, cheerless, and dusky chamber, . . . untenanted so long—except by spiders, and mice, and rats, and ghosts—" that it is "all overgrown with the desolation, which watches to obliterate every trace of man's happier hours." The Pyncheon sundial—*"nullas horas nisi serenas numero"*—has had little traffic with this room, yet in half an hour

Phoebe has "fully succeeded in throwing a kindly and hospitable smile over" it, which has heretofore resembled "nothing so much as the Old Maid's heart," for there is "neither sunshine nor household-fire in one nor the other, and, save for ghosts and ghostly reminiscences, not a guest, for many years gone-by," has entered "the heart or the chamber."

Hepzibah, the chamber's counterpart, has honest compunctions about allowing the youthful Phoebe to remain: " '. . . this house of mine is but a melancholy place for a young person to be in. It lets in the wind and rain—and the snow, too, in the garret and upper chambers, in wintertime—but it never lets in the sunshine! And as for myself, you see what I am; a dismal and lonesome old woman. . . .' " But Phoebe, and the fire that boils the teakettle, are "equally bright, cheerful, and efficient, in their respective offices." The girl has "the cheeriness of an active temperament, finding joy in its activity, and therefore rendering it beautiful." It is "a New England trait—the stern old stuff of Puritanism, with a gold thread in the web." The old china tea set which Hepzibah is now so far enlivened as to bring out, re-echoes this combination in its figures. The "pictured people" are "odd humorists, in a world of their own; a world of vivid brilliancy," as far as color goes, and "still unfaded." Hepzibah's approval of her young relative is conveyed in terms reminiscent of another relative, the Judge, but in a mirror image of him, with the arrangement of the elements reversed. She is "smiling, and, at the same time, frowning so prodigiously" that the smile is "sunshine under a thunder-cloud."

Phoebe is a tempered light and a delicate bloom, softly

touched by the sun and the wind; she represents an ideal moderation. She shocks "no canon of taste"; she is "admirably in keeping with herself" and never jars against "surrounding circumstances." She

> would hardly have suited one's idea of a countess. Neither did her face—with the brown ringlets on either side, and the slightly piquant nose, and the wholesome bloom, and the clear shade of tan, and the half a dozen freckles, friendly remembrancers of the April sun and breeze—precisely give us a right to call her beautiful. But there was both lustre and depth, in her eyes. She was very pretty; as graceful as a bird, and graceful much in the same way; as pleasant about the house, as a gleam of sunshine falling on the floor through a shadow of twinkling leaves, or as a ray of firelight that dances on the wall, while evening is drawing nigh.

Phoebe would have been the ideal woman in a society where ladies did not exist and where "it should be woman's office to move in the midst of practical affairs, and to gild them all . . . with an atmosphere of loveliness and joy." The author remarks:

> It really seemed as if the battered visage of the House of the Seven Gables, black and heavy-browed as it still certainly looked, must have shown a kind of cheerfulness glimmering through its dusky windows, as Phoebe passed to-and-fro in the interior.

The "dusky terror" of Colonel Pyncheon's frown still lingers in the house, but Hepzibah looks upon her young relative "with a grim, yet kindly smile."

Phoebe next exercises her beneficent influence upon the dark and time-soiled Pyncheon garden, which contains the ambiguous well (Chapter VI, "Maule's Well"). The house lowers over it:

> Three of the seven gables either fronted, or looked sideways, with a dark solemnity of aspect, down into the garden. . . . The black, rich soil had fed itself with the decay of a long period of time. . . . The evil of these departed years would naturally have sprung up again, in such rank weeds (symbolic of the transmitted vice of society) as are always prone to root themselves about human dwellings.

Yet the garden has the blessing of nature upon it, along with some signs of human cultivation, which can hardly be the work of Hepzibah, with her "tendency to shelter herself within the dismal shadow of the house." It has an unexpected charm, and "the eye of Heaven" seems to look down into it, "pleasantly, and with a peculiar smile."

Here Phoebe comes upon the daguerreotypist Holgrave. Like her influence, his is positive, though more complicated. It is he who has been tending to the garden, and like her he is associated with sunlight: " 'In short, I make pictures out of sunshine; and, not to be too much dazzled with my own trade, I have prevailed with Miss Hepzibah to let me lodge in one of these dusky gables.' " His is a harder and a drier light than Phoebe's; she remarks that " 'I don't much like pictures of that sort—they are so hard and stern.' " He affirms in reply:

> "Most of my likenesses do look unamiable; but the very sufficient reason, I fancy, is, because the originals are so. There is a wonderful insight in heaven's broad and simple sunshine. While we give it credit only for depicting the merest surface, it actually brings out the secret character

with a truth that no painter would ever venture upon, even could he detect it."

Referring to a portrait of the Judge that he has lately taken, Holgrave says:

"... the original wears, to the world's eye ... an exceedingly pleasant countenance, indicative of benevolence, openness of heart, sunny good humor, and other praiseworthy qualities of that cast. The sun, as you see, tells quite another story, and will not be coaxed out of it, after half a dozen patient attempts on my part."

Phoebe has seen another miniature in the house; it is a portrait of Clifford Pyncheon, though she does not yet realize it. " 'If the original is still in the world, I think he might defy the sun to make him look stern and hard.' " As the two part, Holgrave pays a tribute to Phoebe's attributes of light and bloom. " 'Any bright day, if you will put one of those rose buds in your hair, and come to my rooms in Central-street, I will seize the purest ray of sunshine, and make a picture of the flower and its wearer.' "

Phoebe is very soon to meet the original of the miniature, though he is actually neither very visible nor very audible. An image of Hepzibah herself prepares us for him: in the dark parlor of the house, her "form, though its sable outline" mingles with the dusk, is now "less imperfectly visible." Her darkness, indeed, has its own reality. Clifford is, however, so indistinct that Phoebe hears his voice as a "strange, vague murmur, which might be likened to an indistinct shadow of human utterance."

The next morning is more propitious, with Phoebe lending her own light to it (Chapter VII, "The Guest"). In "the dewy youth of the day" her Indian cakes are "the sweetest offering of all—in their hue, befitting the rustic altars of the innocent and golden age—or, so brightly yellow" are they, "resembling some of the bread which was changed to glistening gold, when Midas tried to eat it." She gathers flowers and arranges them in a glass vase, and the early sunshine, "as fresh as that which peeped into Eve's bower, while she and Adam sat at breakfast there," comes "twinkling through the branches of the pear-tree" and falls "quite across the table." Poor Hepzibah's nervous agitation is so powerful that Phoebe can see "the quivering of her gaunt shadow, as thrown by the firelight on the kitchen-wall, or by the sunshine on the parlor-floor." As in other scenes, Hepzibah's trembling has a mixed significance: she feels an "unwonted joy," which is replaced by "a cold, spectral sorrow, . . . a sorrow as black" as her joy is bright.

Arousing in Phoebe "a sunny and tearful sympathy," she adjures the girl to let in her brightness upon the unfortunate Clifford; but cautiously and gradually:

> "Let him see you first, Phoebe; for you are young and rosy, and cannot help letting a smile break out, whether or no. He always liked bright faces! And mine is old now, and the tears are hardly dry on it. He never could abide tears. There; draw the curtain a little, so that the shadow may fall across his side of the table! But let there be a good deal of sunshine, too; for he never was fond of gloom, as some people are. He has had but little sunshine in his life,—poor Clifford,— and, oh, what a black shadow!"

When the shadowy Clifford appears, he does indeed receive light:

He saw Phoebe . . . and caught an illumination from her youthful and pleasant aspect, which, indeed, threw a cheerfulness about the parlor, like the circle of reflected brilliancy around the glass vase of flowers that was standing in the sunshine.

Clifford is a "wasted, gray, and melancholy figure—a substantial emptiness, a material ghost," but the light is lit, though dimly. A "flickering taper-gleam" in his eyes, which reveals that his "spiritual part" has returned, is "doing its best to kindle the heart's household-fire, and light up intellectual lamps in the dark and ruinous mansion," where it is "doomed to be a forlorn inhabitant."

Clifford is wearing an old damask dressing gown, as in the youthful portrait which Phoebe has already seen. It is now an "old, faded garment, with all its pristine brilliancy extinct," and thus a fitting emblem of its wearer. Yet two earlier images combine with it to elicit hope from its former brilliance: the carpet on the floor in the Colonel's room, where Clifford now resides, a carpet "originally of rich texture, but so worn and faded, in these latter years, that its once brilliant figure" has "quite vanished into one indistinguishable hue" (Chapter II, "The Little Shop-Window"); and the china tea set, already described, with its "world of vivid brilliancy . . . still unfaded."

Clifford is a man of delicate and exquisite taste, a "sybarite" who can be satisfied only by harmonious and modulated effects. It is perceptible, "even there, in the dark, old parlor, in the inevitable polarity" with which his eyes are "attracted towards the quivering play of sunbeams through the shadowy foliage." It is seen in his "appreciating notice of the vase of flowers." And Phoebe combines both. It is "betrayed in the unconscious smile" with which he regards Phoebe, whose "fresh and maidenly figure" is "both sunshine and flowers, their essence, in a prettier and more agreeable mode of manifestation." Long in darkness, he is avid for light,

> vexing the fair moment with a struggle for some added brilliancy and more durable illusion. . . . "How beautiful that play of sunshine! Those flowers, how very fragrant! That young girl's face, how cheerful, how blooming; a flower with the dew on it, and sunbeams in the dew-drops! Ah; this must be all a dream! A dream! A dream! But it has quite hidden the four stone-walls!"

It is, of course, no dream but an awakening, from which Clifford inevitably recedes into somnolence and darkness:

> A slumberous veil diffused itself over his countenance, and had an effect, morally speaking, on its naturally delicate and elegant outline, like that which a brooding mist, with no sunshine in it, throws over the features of a landscape.

He sleeps, and the watching Hepzibah lets down the curtain over the "sunny window" and leaves Clifford to slumber there.

In Chapter VIII, "The Pyncheon of To-day," the Judge, who has hitherto played a walk-on part only, now makes a full appearance. He is "dressed in a black suit of some thin stuff," and "a gold-headed cane of rare, oriental wood adds to the "high respectability of his aspect" as do also "a white neckcloth of the utmost snowy purity, and the conscientious polish of his boots." He has a "dark, square countenance" with an "almost shaggy depth of eyebrows," but he has "considerately taken upon himself to mitigate the harsh effect by a look of exceeding good-humor and benevolence." An acute observer "would probably suspect, that the smile on the gentleman's face was a good deal akin to the shine on his boots, and that each must have cost him and his boot-black, respectively, a good deal of hard labor to bring out and preserve them."

As the Judge enters Hepzibah's little shop, his smile grows "as intense as if he had set his heart on counteracting the whole gloom of the atmosphere . . . by the unassisted light of his countenance." Encountering Phoebe, "a young rosebud of a girl," and learning that she is his relative, he tries to salute her with a cousinly kiss. Involuntarily she draws back; his "glowing benignity," especially in combination with his "dark, full-fed physiognomy," is too intense for her. Indeed, Judge Pyncheon is compacted of excessive and jarring contrasts, false in his sum total, while Phoebe is moderate, harmonious, and true—the genuine light of the sun, which instinctively repudiates its counterfeit.

Rebuffed, the Judge is suddenly and violently transformed. The change is as striking "as that betwixt a landscape under a broad sunshine, and just before a thunderstorm"; not that it has the passionate intensity of the latter aspect," but is "cold, hard, immitigable, like a day-long brooding cloud." Phoebe suddenly realizes that he is the original of Holgrave's photograph and that "the hard, stern relentless look, now on his face" is the same one that the sun "had so inflexibly persisted in bringing out." Recovering his poise, the Judge beams upon Phoebe once more, so that she finds herself "quite overpowered by the sultry, dog-day heat, as it were, of benevolence" which "this excellent man" diffuses out of "his great heart into the surrounding atmosphere." Hawthorne re-emphasizes the general point with a figure that is emblem-like, as if from a bestiary. The Judge is "very much like a serpent, which, as a preliminary to fascination, is said to fill the air with his peculiar odor."

Judge Pyncheon is a throwback to his ancestor the Colonel. His face has lost "the ruddy English hue, that showed its warmth through all the duskiness of the Colonel's weather-beaten cheek," but he outshines the original Pyncheon's "rough heartiness." He has "etherealized this rude benevolence into that broad benignity of smile" with which he shines like a noonday sun along the streets" or glows "like a household fire, in the drawing-rooms of his private acquaintance." At present he continues to shine upon Phoebe, "again beaming sunshine out of his face," until she seems to oppose his way into the house, which he wishes to enter unannounced. Then he addresses her "in a voice as deep as a thunder-growl, and with a frown as black as the cloud whence it issues."

Confronting the formidable Judge, poor Hepzibah is driven by fear and defiance into the appearance of evil. She looks "like the dragon which, in fairy tales, is wont to be the guardian over an enchanted beauty," and her habitual scowl is "undeniably, too fierce . . . to pass itself off on the innocent score of nearsightedness." She takes on, indeed, the true aspect of her adversary, which he in turn conceals "with a smile, so broad and sultry, that, had it been only half as warm as it looked, a trellis of grapes might at once have turned purple under its summer-like exposure." The Judge's true nature is made wholly evident very shortly. At the sound of Clifford's voice he becomes a beast of prey:

> A red fire kindled in his eyes; and he made a quick pace forward, with something inexpressibly fierce and grim, darkening forth, as it were, out of the whole man. To know Judge Pyncheon, was to see him at that moment. After such a revelation, let him smile with what sultriness he would, he could much sooner turn grapes purple, or pumpkins yellow, than melt the iron-branded impression out of the beholder's memory.

Again he conceals himself, however, and "an all-comprehensive benignity blazes from his visage." Indeed, at his departure, "smiling along the street,"

> so excessive was the warmth of Judge Pyncheon's kindly aspect, that (such, at least, was the rumor about town) an extra passage of the water-carts was found essential, in order to lay the dust occasioned by so much extra sunshine!

Hepzibah, overwhelmed by misfortune and the shadow of the house, cannot of herself resuscitate her moribund brother, Clifford. She tries to entertain him by reading aloud to him, but her voice is "a kind of croak," the effect of "a settled melancholy, . . . as if the voice had been dyed black" (Chapter IX, "Clifford and Phoebe"). She can only brood upon him with a "dark anxiety." It thus devolves upon the bright Phoebe to rekindle his spirits: "Phoebe's presence, and the contiguity of her fresh life to his blighted one," is usually all that he requires. Vitality emanates from her: such is "the native gush and play of her spirit" that she is "seldom perfectly quiet and undemonstrative, any more than a fountain ever ceases to dimple and warble with its flow." She sings with surpassing naturalness, she is spontaneity itself:

> So long as Phoebe sang, she might stray at her own will about the house. Clifford was content, whether the sweet, airy homeliness of her tones came down from the upper chambers, or along the passageway from the shop, or was sprinkled through the foliage of the peartree, inward from the garden, with the twinkling sunbeams. He would sit quietly, with a gentle pleasure gleaming over his face, brighter now, and now a little dimmer, as the song happened to float near him, or was more remotely heard.

Amid this synesthetic play of natural sound and light and fluidity, the "homeliness" is significant and characteristic of Hawthorne. Characteristic too of Phoebe, her song is tempered with pathos, and thus the more fitting in decorum for the situation of Clifford and Hepzibah and "the sacred presence of dark misfortune." This pathos comes "sifted through the golden texture of a cheery spirit" and is "somehow so interfused with the quality thence acquired" that the heart feels "all the lighter for having wept at it."

To this light the sensitive Clifford is most receptive:

> A beauty—not precisely real . . . beauty, nevertheless, that was not a mere dream, would sometimes play upon and illuminate his face. It did more than to illuminate; it transfigured him with an expression that could only be interpreted as the glow of an exquisite and happy spirit.

The glow is as transient as it is exquisite, and age comes stealing, "like a sad twilight, back over his figure." Thus

Phoebe adds to her beauty and harmony, essential to Clifford as a lover of "the Beautiful," the greatest gift of all, her reality:

> She was real! Holding her hand, you felt something; a tender something; a substance, and a warm one; and so long as you should feel its grasp, soft as it was, you might be certain that your place was good in the whole sympathetic chain of human nature. The world was no longer a delusion.

We recall that Clifford has been depicted as an almost impalpable shadow, an almost inaudible voice.

Phoebe has no special comprehension of what is subtle and extraordinary in Clifford. Her influence upon him is simple, sunlike, vitally natural. The path "which would best suit her is "the well-worn track of ordinary life," and the mystery enveloping Clifford, what is "darkly picturesque in his situation," has no appeal to her sunny spirit. In her "native kindliness" she gives him warmth, "purer air," impregnated "not with a wild-flower scent," for wildness is "no trait of hers," but "with the perfume of garden-roses, pinks, and other blossoms of much sweetness, which nature and man have consented together in making grow, from summer to summer, and from century to century." As a flower, she droops a little in "the heavy atmosphere about her." She grows thoughtful at the spectacle of Clifford's "dim, unsatisfactory elegance," questioning whether the veil that surrounds him is from birth itself or a "gray texture woven of some dark calamity." Symptomatically, he dozes every morning; unless he is accidentally disturbed, he does not emerge from a "dense cloud of slumber, or the thinner mists" that flit to and fro, until noon. It is dark Hepzibah's task to watch over his slumbers, but when he wakes, it is "the young girl's turn" to oversee his brighter hours.

In Chapter X ("The Pyncheon Garden") Clifford is roused by "Phoebe's more active instigation" from the "torpor" which has "crept through all his modes of being" to accompany her to the garden, where Uncle Venner and Holgrave have "made such repairs on the roof of the ruinous arbor, or summer-house" that it is now a "sufficient shelter from sunshine and casual showers," a "green play-place of flickering light." In this garden retreat, as the girl reads to Clifford, she is often conscious from his face "that a more delicate intelligence than her own" has caught "a lambent flame" from what she reads. "One glow of this kind," however, is often "the precursor of gloom, for many hours afterward." Clifford is enjoying "a kind of Indian summer, with a mist in its balmiest sunshine, and decay and death in its gaudiest delight." He seems to "taste the happiness of a child," but since he is not a child, his state is divided and inharmonious.

He likes to "hang over Maule's Well, and look at the constantly shifting phantasmagoria of figures, produced by the agitation of the water over the mosaic work of colored pebbles, at the bottom." There he sees faces, "beautiful faces, arrayed in bewitching smiles—each momentary face so fair and rosy, and every smile so sunny" that he feels "wronged at its departure, until the same flitting witchcraft" makes a new one. But sometimes he suddenly cries out: " 'The dark face gazes at me!' " and is "miserable, the whole day afterwards." It is explained that his fancy, "reviving faster than his will and judgement, and always stronger than they," creates "shapes of loveliness" that are "symbolic of his native character, and now and then a stern and dreadful shape" that typifies his fate. At a peaceful Sunday-afternoon party in the garden, in "the yellow richness of the declining sunshine," Clifford is the gayest of the company. He is responsive to what is said around him and gives out "his own thoughts, likewise, with an airy and fanciful glow," so that they glisten, "as it were, through the arbor," and make their escape "among the interstices of the foliage." But as the sunlight leaves the peaks of the seven gables, so does the excitement "fade out of Clifford's eyes. . . . 'I want my happiness!'" he murmurs, "hoarsely and indistinctly, hardly shaping out the words." Yet he has such happiness as he can well expect already: "If not the thing itself, it is marvellously like it, and the more so for that ethereal and intangible quality, which causes it all to vanish, at too close an introspection."

Looking out upon the world, the unaccustomed Clifford is struck with wonder at many common sights (Chapter XI, "The Arched Window"). He gazes out from the vantage point of the window, meanwhile himself concealed and "peering from behind the faded crimson of the curtain," in a manner reminiscent of Dimmesdale at Governor Bellingham's mansion. Some quite customary things Clifford's mind will not retain; for example, he never becomes accustomed to the water cart that goes by the house two or three times "during the sunny hours of the day, . . . leaving a broad wake of moistened earth, instead of the white dust. . . ." It is "like a summer-shower." The scene, trivial and matter-of-fact as it appears to be, fits the sun-and-shower pattern noted earlier, and a more general pattern of alternation and moderation that goes beyond *The House of the Seven Gables*. Commonplace reality has to be faced, but one is not obliged to submit entirely to its aridity. As for the forgetful Clifford, he loses "the recollection of this perambulatory shower, before its next reappearance, as completely" as does the street itself, along which the heat so quickly strews "white dust" again.

Some experiences Clifford enjoys for their liveliness—even discordances, such as the scissors-grinder's wheel. It makes "an ugly, little venomous serpent of a noise," but it has "very brisk life in it," and as Clifford and a circle of curious children watch the revolutions of the wheel, it appears to give him "a more vivid sense of active, bustling, and sunshiny existence" than he has attained "in almost any other way." It is remarked, however, that its charm lies "chiefly in the past; for the scissor-grinder's wheel had hissed in his childish ears."

Clifford looks out at life in an instinctive attempt to rejoin it. His deepest and most dangerous commitment comes from the sight of a political procession. A procession, perceived as a whole, is

> one great life—one collected body of mankind, with a vast, homogeneous spirit animating it. . . . an impressible person, standing alone over the brink of one of these processions, should behold it . . . in its aggregate—as a mighty river of life, massive in its tide, and black with mystery, and, out of its depths, calling to the kindred depth within him. . . . It might so fascinate him, that he would hardly be restrained from plunging into the surging stream of human sympathies.

Clifford is an impressible person, and he is restrained just in time by Hepzibah and Phoebe from plunging into the black river that flows beneath him, an ambiguous river of life that may also be a Lethe of death. At his action Phoebe, to whom all extravagance is "a horror," bursts into "sobs and tears."

In "a similar yearning to renew the broken links of brotherhood," Clifford thinks of going to church. Like the Ancient Mariner, he would like

To walk together to the kirk
With a goodly company.

To this he is prompted by "one of those bright, calm Sabbaths, with its own hallowed atmosphere, when Heaven seems to diffuse itself over the earth's face in a solemn smile, no less sweet than solemn," when "the air, with God's sweetest and tenderest sunshine in it," is "meet for mankind to breathe into their hearts, and send it forth again as the utterance of prayer." He watches the neighbors from his window as they step into the street. As she leaves the house, Phoebe puts up her sunshade and throws upward "a glance and smile of parting kindness to the faces at the arched window." But when Clifford and Hepzibah seek to follow, they can barely cross the threshold of the house, feeling as if they are "standing in the presence of the whole world, and with mankind's great and terrible eye on them alone." "The eye of their Father" seems to be withdrawn, and gives them no encouragement. "The warm, sunny air of the street" makes them shiver. Rebuffed and defeated, they shrink back into the "dusky passage-way" and close the door.

Clifford is not ready to face the broad sunshine of reality, whether humor or divine. He needs and receives protection from it by regressing to his childhood, in dreams where "the nightly moonshine" interweaves itself with "the morning mist" and envelops him "as in a robe," which he hugs about his person and seldom lets realities "pierce through." He cannot endure his identity as a broken, aging man. One afternoon he takes refuge in blowing soap bubbles, "little, impalpable worlds, . . . with the big world depicted, in hues bright as imagination, on the nothing of their surface." As fate would have it, just as Judge Pyncheon happens to be passing, a large bubble sails down and bursts against his nose. The Judge looks up, first with "a stern, keen glance" and "then with a smile, which might be conceived as diffusing a dog-day sultriness for the space of several yards about him."

Childlike, Clifford usually lies down to rest while the sunbeams are "still melting through his window-curtains" or are "thrown with late lustre on the chamber-wall." Discussing him with Holgrave (Chapter XII, "The Daguerreotypist"), Phoebe reflects that " 'his humor changes without any reason that can be guessed at, just as a cloud comes over the sun.' " She feels, however, that it is " 'not quite right to look closely into his moods. . . . When he is cheerful—when the sun shines into his mind—then I venture to peep in, just as far as the light reaches, but no further. It is holy ground where the shadow falls!' " The dark, more analytical Holgrave " 'can understand the feeling, without possessing it.' " Nevertheless, he turns the conversation "to themes less dark."

Holgrave, despite "premature experience of life," has not "wasted entirely that beautiful spirit of youth, which, gushing forth from one small heart and fancy, may diffuse itself over the universe, making it all as bright as on the first day of creation." This is in itself good:

> When, with the years settling down more weightily upon him, his early faith should be modified by inevitable experience, . . . he would still have faith in man's brightening destiny. . . . The haughty faith, with which he began life, would be well bartered for a far humbler one, at its close, in discerning that man's best-directed effort accomplishes a kind of dream, while God is the sole worker of realities.

Holgrave, in fact, promises fairly, though we are soberly cautioned that "his career it would be difficult to prefigure." Many bright young men deceive themselves and others. "Like certain chintzes, calicoes, and ginghams, they show finely in their first newness, but cannot stand the sun and rain, and assume a very sober aspect after washing-day."

Holgrave, a descendant of the submerged and almost forgotten Maules, carries with him some of their darkness, though he has in the main escaped it. The story of "Alice Pyncheon" (Chapter XIII) that he now tells to Phoebe (" 'among the multitude of my marvellous gifts, I have that of writing stories' ") is not a tale for open daylight. He begins it "while the late sunbeams" gild the seven gables, a narrative of Pyncheon pride and the dark powers of the injured Maules that is set some thirty-seven years after the birth of the house and the mysterious death of its founder, the Colonel. The tale requires little attention here, but it does possess the patterns of sunlight and darkness.

The vengeful, brooding Matthew Maule carries with him the shadow of his injury and his dangerous gifts of wizardry. " 'What for,' " asks the Pyncheon's black servant, " 'do you look so black at me?' " Later, as Maule talks with Gervayse Pyncheon, "a dark smile," several times mentioned, makes "a riddle of his countenance." In involving Alice Pyncheon in their business, he gives her father to understand, "in a mysterious kind of explanation," which makes the matter considerably "darker" than it has looked before, that "the only chance of acquiring the requisite knowledge" is "through the clear, crystal medium of a pure and virgin intelligence." When at last he has unintentionally destroyed Alice in his efforts to humiliate her, he is "the darkest and woefullest man that ever walked behind a corpse." His grandfather, the original Maule, is held by popular superstition to rise from his grave and is "as often seen at midnight, as living people at noonday." His grandson's spells succeed in evoking him as "an aged man, meanly dressed, with a dark and malign countenance." The house has still, as in its infancy, "glittering plaster-work," which sparkles in the October sun, "as if it had been new only a week ago," and its sundial is still there. But to the eyes of the gloomy Maule, " 'the shadow creeps and creeps, and is always looking over the shoulder of the sunshine!' " Also the fateful survey map is "now dingy with smoke, and soiled, here and there, with the touch of fingers."

Chapter XIV, "Phoebe's Good-Bye," casts another sort of light upon the subject, the moonlight of imagination and sympathy, perhaps appropriate to Holgrave's artistry in romance, and appropriate also to the growing attach-

ment between himself and Phoebe, now definitely signalized. (It is to be noted that he has resisted the temptation to
assume control over Phoebe through the accidental effects
of his miming, as he imitates the gestures by which Matthew Maule hypnotized Alice Pyncheon.) By the end of
the story the sun has gone down and is "tinting the clouds
towards the zenith with those bright hues, which are not
seen there until some time after sunset, and when the hori-
zon has quite lost its richer brilliancy." Twilight, frequently the setting for Hawthorne's tales, is most characteristically the light, tone, and atmosphere of his romantic art,
between the sun and the moon, and partaking of both. The
rising moon, in a passage quoted earlier in this chapter,
lends picturesqueness to the garden with a point of view
more selective than sunshine.

So "sweetly cool" is the atmosphere "that the summer
eve might be fancied as sprinkling dews and liquid moonlight, with a dash of icy temper in them, out of a silver
vase." Touched by its influence, Holgrave momentarily
perceives the time-worn house and the corrupted soil of
the garden as " 'a bower in Eden, blossoming with the
earliest roses that God ever made. Moonlight, and the
sentiment in man's heart, responsive to it, are the greatest
of renovators and reformers. He reflects that " 'all other
reform and renovation, I suppose, will prove to be no
better than moonshine!' " The sunny Phoebe, who has
" 'never cared much about moonlight before,' " is also
responsive to its spell. " 'It seems,' " she says, " 'as if I had
looked at everything, hitherto, in broad daylight, or else
in the ruddy light of a cheerful fire, glimmering and dancing through a room.' " Life with the melancholy Hepzibah

and the shattered Clifford has subdued her. " 'I have given them my sunshine, and have been glad to give it; but, of course, I cannot both give and keep it.' "

This Eden is, then, not the first Eden of first youth but a renewal. " 'Our first youth is of no value,' " Holgrave philosophizes, " 'for we are never conscious of it, until after it is gone. But sometimes . . . there comes a sense of second youth, gushing out of the heart's joy at being in love; or, possibly, it may come to crown some other grand festival in life, if any other such there be.' " He continues, " 'This bemoaning of one's self (as you do now) over the first, careless, shallow gaiety of youth departed, and this profound happiness at youth regained—so much deeper and richer than that we lost—are essential to the soul's development.' "

The scene is a climax to the peaceful days of gradual amelioration enjoyed by the house in the sunny reign of Phoebe. Now she is about to depart, though temporarily, and gloomier days lie in prospect. " 'I cannot help fancying that Destiny is arranging its fifth act for a catastrophe,' " says Holgrave—to Phoebe's vexation, for she is "by nature as hostile to mystery, as the sunshine to a dark corner." She finds herself "more regretful at leaving this spot of black earth, vitiated with such an age-long growth of weeds, than joyful at the idea of again scenting her pine-forests and fresh clover-fields." Hepzibah encourages her to go: " 'The house is too gloomy and lonesome; the shop is full of vexations; and as for me, I have no faculty of making things look brighter than they are.' " Clifford's delicate insight detects a deeper change within her: " '. . . you have deepened into beauty! Girlhood has passed into womanhood; the bud is a bloom!' " Old Uncle Venner warns her that she is essential to the dwellers of the house. " 'Don't it seem to you they'd be in a sad case, if, some pleasant summer morning like this, the angel should spread his wings, and fly to the place he came from? Well; just so they feel, now that you're going home by the railroad!' " Like an angel, or perhaps more like Aurora of the dawn, Phoebe takes "the wings of the morning" and is "soon flitting almost as rapidly away as if endowed with the aerial locomotion of the angels" to whom Uncle Venner has "so graciously compared her."

With Phoebe gone, an easterly storm sets in; the time of the Judge has arrived. Phoebe is not there, nor does "the sunshine fall upon the floor." Hepzibah appears to be, "in her very person, only another phase of this gray and sullen spell of weather; the East Wind itself, grim and disconsolate, in a rusty black silk-gown, and with a turban of cloud-wreaths on its head!" She tries "to enliven matters by a fire in the parlor. But the "storm-demon" keeps watch above and, whenever a flame is kindled, drives the smoke back again, "choking the chimney's sooty throat with its own breath." Clifford, after a struggle, finally takes to his bed in despair. The Judge, when he arrives, has disguised himself as usual, and it is Hepzibah who seems the genius of the storm. "Few of her sex, on such occasions, have ever looked so terrible as our poor scowling Hepzibah" (Chapter XV, "The Scowl and Smile"), whereas the Judge is able to summon "a visage of composed benignity, to meet the alarm and anger" his appearance has excited. It seems "wonderful, . . . indeed, that the easterly storm" is not "put to shame, or, at any rate, a little mollified, by the genial benevolence of his smile." When, however, his purpose of seeing Clifford is opposed, "the very frown of the old Puritan" darkens through the room as he speaks. Hepzibah taxes him with cherishing " 'at this moment, some black purpose against him, in your heart.' "

Few share Hepzibah's opinion of her kinsman, and the Judge's own conscience is at rest, "unless it might be for the little space of five minutes in the twenty-four hours, or, now and then, some black day in the whole year's circle." Men of his kind delude themselves, not with Clifford's shimmering bubbles, but with "the big, heavy, solid un-realities, such as gold, landed estate, offices of trust and emolument, and public honors." Such an individual builds for himself a palace, whose windows "admit the sunshine through the most transparent of plate-glass . . . . With what fairer and nobler emblem could any man desire to shadow forth his character?" Yet "in some low and ob-scure nook,—some narrow closet, . . . or beneath the marble pavement . . . may lie a corpse, half-decayed, and still decaying, and diffusing its death-scent all through the palace!" Common visitors sense nothing of this, but

> Now and then, perchance, comes in a seer, before whose sadly gifted eye the whole structure melts into thin air, leaving only the hidden nook, the bolted closet, with the cobwebs festooned over its forgotten door, or the deadly hole under the pavement, and the decaying corpse within.

The "splendid rubbish" of the Judge's life, his "smile of broad benevolence," appears to leave no room in his portrait for "darker traits." Yet when he is defied by Hepzibah, the true man is revealed, a Satan:

. . . his look assumed sternness, the sense of power, and immitigable resolve; . . . it seemed as if the iron man had stood there from the first, and the meek man not at all. The effect was as when the light, vapory clouds, with their soft coloring, suddenly vanish from the stony brow of a precipitous mountain, and leave there the frown which you at once feel to be eternal.

He enforces his demands with a "harsh frown," while his brow grows "almost a black purple, in the shadow of the room."

Never has the old house appeared so dismal to poor Hepzibah as when she goes on the "wretched errand" of summoning Clifford to the Judge. The legends of the Pyncheons, "which had heretofore been kept warm in her remembrance by the chimney-corner glow," now recur to her, "sombre, ghastly, cold, like most passages of family history, when brooded over in melancholy mood." Gazing from the arched window, she is shocked to realize that all is the same, "except for the difference between sunshine and sullen storm." Coming again to the window, she lifts her eyes, scowling, "poor, dim-sighted Hepzibah, in the face of Heaven!" and tries hard to send up a prayer through the "dense, gray pavement of clouds." The clouds have gathered "as if to symbolize a great, brooding mass of human trouble, doubt, confusion, and chill indifference, between earth and the better regions." It is useless to pray, for Providence does not deal with individuals but sheds "its justice, and its mercy, in a broad, sunlike sweep, over half the universe at once." Hepzibah does not see that, "just as there comes a warm sunbeam into every cottage-window, so comes a love-beam of God's care and pity, for every separate need" (Chapter XVI, "Clifford's Chamber").

Unable to find her brother, she wonders whether he has strayed outside and perhaps taken refuge "under the cheerless shelter of the summer-house." Finally she turns back in desperation to the waiting Judge. "But, what with the shade of branches across the windows, and the smoke-blackened ceiling, and the dark oak-panelling of the walls," there is "hardly so much daylight in the room that Hepzibah's imperfect sight" can "accurately distinguish the Judge's figure." Thus ironically he duplicates in his death the nullity of Clifford when he first shadowily appears to Phoebe's eyes in the same room. Clifford himself now appears again, this time clearly visible and in another irony reproducing the pallor of the dead man. Clifford's face is "preternaturally pale; so deadly white, indeed, that, through all the glimmering indistinctness of the passage-way," Hepzibah can clearly discern his features, as though a light is falling directly on them.

As, stupefied by the event, the two flee the house (Chapter XVII, "The Flight of Two Owls"), they merge with their dark surroundings. "Had it been a sunny and cheerful day" they would have been noticed. As it is, they are probably felt to be "in keeping with the dismal and bitter weather" and therefore do not "stand out in strong relief, as if the sun were shining on them," but melt into the "gray gloom," and are "forgotten as soon as gone." Correspondingly, in Hepzibah's bemusement, "the feeling of indistinctness and unreality" keeps "dimly hovering round-about her, and so diffusing itself into her system" that one of her hands is "hardly palpable to the touch of the other."

When under Clifford's sway she boards a train with him, the motion adds to this sense of the unreal: The "spires of meeting-houses" seem "set adrift from their foundations"; the "broad-based hills" glide away. Everything is "unfixed from its age-long rest, and moving at whirlwind speed in a direction opposite to their own."

Meanwhile Clifford, escaping from the house, is for the moment highly exhilarated. He catches the "color" of what is passing about him and throws it back "more vividly than he received it, but mixed, nevertheless, with a lurid and portentous hue." As he converses, his countenance glows. A "youthful character" shines out from within, "converting the wrinkles and pallid duskiness of age into an almost transparent mask." Yet the house of the seven gables runs obsessively through all he says, and the figure of the dead Judge Pyncheon. Wildly theorizing, he says, " 'It is as clear to me as sunshine' " that houses should be abolished. " 'The soul needs air; a wide sweep and frequent change of it.' " In contrast, there is " 'a certain house within my familiar recollection . . . a rusty, crazy, creaky, dry-rotted, damp-rotted, dingy, dark, and miserable old dungeon.' " Inside it a dead man sits in a chair.

At the thought, Clifford's face darkens, and seems to "contract, and shrivel itself up, and wither into age." He keeps coming back to it: "a great, gloomy, dark-chambered mansion" and "a dark, low, cross-beamed, panelled room of an old house" in which a dead man sits in an armchair, "with a blood-stain on his shirt-bosom." Finally, it is the sight of "a wooden church, black with age," and "a farm-house in the old style, as venerably black as the church," that destroys "the wild effervescence" of Clifford's mood and stays the journey. No real escape from the house is attainable by physical flight, and in any event Clifford and Hepzibah cannot redeem themselves unaided. Burdened with the responsibility of decision, Hepzibah kneels down upon the platform and lifts her clasped hands to the sky. "The dull, gray weight of clouds" makes the sky invisible, but it is no "hour for disbelief"—no time to question that there is a "sky above, and an Almighty Father looking down from it!"

The story now moves, "like an owl, bewildered in the daylight" to the house of the dead Judge, foreshadowing the return of Clifford and Hepzibah (Chapter XVIII, "Governor Pyncheon"). The chapter is an ironic meditation on time and the eternity into which the dead man has entered. Time passes, minute by minute, and with it the Judge's carefully organized commitments, including the political dinner which would have made him the next governor of Massachusetts. Night comes and slowly passes into morning; the wind shifts, and the storm is dispelled.

Figuratively, the influence of the Judge broods over the chamber until full darkness. First,

> ... the twilight is glooming upward. ... The shadows of the tall furniture grow deeper, ... spreading wider, they lose their distinctness of outline in the dark, gray tide of oblivion. ... The gloom has not entered from without; it has brooded here all day, and now, taking its own inevitable time, will possess itself of everything.

Only the Judge's white face, like Clifford's earlier, "refuses to melt into this universal solvent." The light changes from gray to sable, and only "the swarthy whiteness—we shall venture to marry these ill-agreeing words—" remains. "The features are all gone; there is only the paleness of them left." Next, total dark: "There is no face! An infinite, inscrutable blackness has annihilated sight! Where is our universe? All crumbled away from us; and we, adrift in chaos, may hearken to the gusts of homeless wind. . . ."

With a change in the wind, light reappears from the stars and the moon, beautiful, but cold, weird, and ambiguous. It mocks the Judge, who is still the center of the scene:

> Observe that silvery dance upon the upper branches of the pear-tree, and now a little lower, and now on the whole mass of boughs, while, through their shifting intricacies, the moonbeams fall aslant into the room. . . . They follow the shadows, in changeful sport, across his unchanging features.

They gleam upon the dial of his watch, which reminds us of the sundial outside.

In the light of the moonbeams the watch reads midnight, though "a man of sturdy understanding, like Judge Pyncheon, cares no more for twelve o'clock at night, than for the corresponding hour of noon." Now, at this traditional hour, the influence of the dead Judge is diffused in a fanciful pageant of the Pyncheons and the Maules. "First comes the ancestor himself, in his black cloak. . . . A frown of deadly import . . . darkens over the shadow of his features, . . . through which, nevertheless, the moonlight passes, and flickers on the wall beyond." Not all are from the past: there is a young man in a dark frock coat, "dressed in the very fashion of to-day." It is the Judge's son, who has predeceased him. Finally, there is the Judge himself, though his corpse is still visible sitting in the chair, "a stout, elderly gentleman . . . of eminent respectability," wearing "a black coat and pantaloons." This is a fantastic, not an actual, scene, suggested by "the quiver of the moonbeams; they dance hand-in-hand with shadows, and are reflected in the looking-glass, which . . . is always a kind of window or door-way into the spiritual world." The night wears away at last, and "gives place to a fresh, transparent, cloudless morn."

"The day-beam—even what little of it finds its way into this always dusky parlor—seems part of the universal benediction, annulling evil, and rendering all goodness possible, and happiness attainable." The Judge will no longer walk the streets, "with that dog-day smile of elaborate benevolence, sultry enough to tempt flies to come and buzz in it. . . . The morning sunshine glimmers through the foliage, and, beautiful and holy as it is, shuns not to kindle up your face." All is indeed transformed. It would be "enough to live for merely to look up at the wide benediction of the sky," or as much of it as is "visible between the houses, genial once more with sunshine." The Pyncheon elm is "full of the morning sun," and one branch of it has been "transmuted to bright gold . . . like the golden branch, that gained Aeneas and the Sybil admittance into Hades." Even the windows of the dark house gleam cheerfully in the "slanting sunlight," as if its history had been "a decorous and happy one, and such as would be delightful for a fireside-tale" (Chapter XIX, "Alice's Posies").

For some time, on this early morning, nature surrounds the house with the benignancy of harmonious light and sound and motion. The elm makes "a pleasant, cheerful, sunny sigh, responsive to the breeze" that is "elsewhere imperceptible"; a swarm of insects buzz merrily under its "drooping shadow" and become "specks of light" when they dart into the sunshine; a locust sings, "once or twice, . . . and a solitary little bird, with plumage of pale gold," hovers about "Alice's Posies." Yet the house, a "silent and impenetrable mansion," is an image of the Pyncheon past and of the Judge himself. Amid the daily business of the town, "the current human life making this small eddy hereabouts," the traffic of deliverymen is like "whirling sticks, straws, and all such trifles, round and round, right over the black depth" where a corpse lies "unseen." The butcher, peering through a curtain, catches a glimpse of "the stalwart legs, clad in black pantaloons, of a man sitting in a large oaken chair." The silence of the house rouses uneasiness. Children take alarm and run away; "looking back at the grotesque peaks and shadowy angles of the old mansion," they fancy "a gloom diffused about it, which no brightness of the sunshine" can dispel. Shortly afterward, however, Phoebe arrives, to signal the breaking of the Pyncheon spell for good, a Phoebe "graver, more womanly and deeper-eyed, in token of a heart" that has begun to "suspect its depths," but still with "the quiet glow of natural sunshine over her."

Entering the house "suddenly from the sunny daylight," Phoebe is "altogether bedimmed in such density of shadow" as lurks in "most of the passages of the old house." Before her eyes have "adapted themselves to the obscurity," a hand grasps hers "with a firm, but gentle and warm pressure, thus imparting a welcome" which causes her heart "to leap and thrill with an undefinable shiver of enjoyment." The hand is Holgrave's, who proceeds to draw her into a room where the sunshine comes "freely into all the uncurtained windows." Although he is "paler than ordinary," his smile of welcome is "full of genuine warmth" and has in it a "joy, by far the most vivid expression" that Phoebe has ever witnessed, "shining out of the New England reserve" with which Holgrave habitually masks his emotions. He has discovered the desertion of Clifford and Hepzibah and the corpse of the Judge. By taking a daguerreotype of the latter he contributes his own kind of sunlight, as it were, to reveal the secret of Judge Pyncheon's death and to clear the unlucky Clifford of suspicion attaching to it. The picture may also go far "towards obliterating the black stain on Clifford's character" from his supposed murder thirty years before of his uncle, who died from the same cause as that which killed the Judge (Chapter XX, "The Flower of Eden").

The two go hand in hand "through a shadow-haunted passage." Characteristically, Phoebe would immediately "throw open the doors," but Holgrave detains her. He has, he avows, been rescued by her in a

> "dark, cold, miserable hour! The presence of yonder dead man threw a great black shadow over everything; he made the universe, so far as my perception could reach, a scene of guilt and of retribution more dreadful than the guilt. The sense of it took away my youth. I never hoped to feel young again! The world looked strange, wild, evil, hostile; my past life, so lonesome and dreary; my future, a shapeless gloom, which I must mould into gloomy shapes! But, Phoebe, you crossed the threshold; and hope, warmth, and

joy, came in with you! The black moment became at once a blissful one. . . . I love you!"

Phoebe confesses her own love for him, and

The bliss, which makes all things true, beautiful, and holy, shone around this youth and maiden. They were conscious of nothing sad nor old. They transfigured the earth, and made it Eden again, and themselves the two first dwellers in it.

Clifford, who has returned, now appears and completes for Phoebe her pattern of light and bloom, and at the same time figuratively redeems at long last the unhappy Alice Pyncheon, her beautiful ancestor. " 'I thought of you both,' " he says, " 'as we came down the street, and beheld Alice's Posies in full bloom. And so the flower of Eden has bloomed, likewise, in this old, darksome house, today!' "

IV. THE BLITHEDALE
ROMANCE

THE *Blithedale Romance* commences with a reference to the Veiled Lady, whose

> misty drapery . . . was white, with somewhat of a subdued silver sheen, like the sunny side of a cloud; and falling over the wearer, from head to foot, was supposed to insulate her from the material world, from time and space, and to endow her with many of the privileges of a disembodied spirit.

This veil, as we shall find, though literally an imposture, is nevertheless a veritable symbol of the being of Priscilla, whom it imprisons yet protects. Its sunniness is the sign of its beneficence, perhaps derived from Priscilla herself. Next, in this book of veils and disguises, the narrator Coverdale, coming upon old Moodie, sees "something characteristic in the old fellow's way of standing under the arch of a gate, only revealing enough of himself to make me recognize him as an acquaintance." Moodie, like Dimmesdale and Clifford, prefers concealment. Last, Zenobia is introduced into their conversation. Her name, remarks Coverdale, is " 'a sort of mask in which she comes before the world, retaining all the privileges of privacy—a contrivance, in short, like the white drapery of the Veiled Lady, only a little more transparent.' "

There is little sunshine in the early chapters of *The Blithedale Romance*. The point of view itself is the chill retrospect of "a frosty bachelor, with another white hair, every week or so, in my mustache" (Chapter II, "Blithedale"). Blithedale, a utopian paradise in prospect, has its end in its beginning, an unseasonable April snowstorm. Its images are darkness and cold, with their logical opposite the genial glow of a wood fire. Even this glow, through Coverdale's gloomy vision, "must be represented, if at all, by the merest phosphoric glimmer, like that which exudes, rather than shines, from damp fragments of decayed trees, deluding the benighted wanderer through a forest." The first night at Blithedale is enlivened by Zenobia, endowed with a "bloom, health, and vigor, which she possessed in such overflow that a man might well have fallen in love with her for their sake only." Zenobia is indeed a fitting Eve for paradise, but she says, " 'I am afraid . . . we shall find some difficulty in adopting the Paradisiacal system, for at least a month to come. . . . As for the garb of Eden, . . . I shall not assume it till after May-day!' " (Chapter III, "A Knot of Dreamers").

Zenobia is potentially a goddess of the sun and bloom, a Flora, a Ceres. It would "have befitted the bounteous nature of this beautiful woman to scatter fresh flowers from her hand, and to revive faded ones by her touch." Yet her light can like the sun be blighting, too harshly real: ". . . the presence of Zenobia caused our heroic enterprise to show like an illusion, a masquerade, a pastoral, a counterfeit Arcadia, in which we grown-up men and women were making a play-day of the years that were given us to live in." Somehow there is always too much of Zenobia, some excess, some failure in the blending of her. The flower she invariably wears comes from a hot-house.

On this same night Priscilla makes her first appearance (Chapter IV, "The Supper-Table"). She is Zenobia's opposite; her face is "of a wan, almost sickly hue, betokening habitual seclusion from the sun and free atmosphere, like a flower-shrub" that has "done its best to blossom in too scanty light." Says Coverdale:

> The fantasy occurred to me that she was some desolate kind of a creature, doomed to wander about in snow-storms, and that, though the ruddiness of window-panes had tempted her into a human dwelling, she would not remain long enough to melt the icicles out of her hair.

Hollingsworth, who has brought the girl to Blithedale, has warmth but not light. He belongs, not in open sunlight, but by the fire of a cave, "with his great shaggy head, . . . his abundant beard." He says of the unknown Priscilla:

> "Let us warm her poor, shivering body with this good fire, and her poor, shivering heart with our best kindness. . . . And, in good time, whatever is desirable for us to know will be melted out of her, as inevitably as those tears which we see now."

Zenobia views Priscilla by the dry sunlight of a common-sense realism (Chapter V, "Until Bedtime"). To an expression of interest from Coverdale she replies:

> "Since you see the young woman in so poetical a light, . . . you had better turn the affair into a ballad. It is a grand sub-

ject, and worthy of supernatural machinery. The storm, the startling knock at the door, the entrance of the sable knight Hollingsworth and this shadowy snow-maiden, who, precisely at the stroke of midnight, shall melt away at my feet in a pool of ice-cold water and give me my death with a pair of wet slippers!"

(This speech is a prophetic one, by the way. It could be said that Priscilla does indeed give Zenobia her death "with a pair of wet slippers.") At length kind to the girl, Zenobia caresses her briefly:

> The touch had a magical effect. So vivid a look of joy flushed up between those fingers, that it seemed as if the sad and wan Priscilla had been snatched away, and another kind of creature substituted in her place.

Priscilla is no longer cold and alone; from that moment she becomes one of them and is no longer a "foreign element."

For the new community Zenobia suggests the name "Sunny Glimpse," as "expressive of a vista into a better system of society," but the name is rejected as too sentimental "for sun-burnt men to work under," and its former name, Blithedale, is retained. The auguries are not favorable. On this first evening,

> ... the outer solitude looked in upon us through the windows, gloomy, wild, and vague, like another state of existence, close beside the littler sphere of warmth and light in which we were the prattlers and bustlers of a moment.

Retiring to bed (with "a tremendous cold"), Coverdale is oppressed by dreams, which, he says in retrospect, "anticipated several of the chief incidents of this narrative, including a dim shadow of its catastrophe." Waking in the night, he sees that the storm is past and that the moon is "shining on the snowy landscape," which looks like a "lifeless copy of the world in marble." This moonlight is equivocal, and "lifeless copy" is positively ominous. Furthermore, "from the bank of the distant river," which is "shimmering in the moonlight," comes the "black shadow of the only cloud in heaven." This cloud, perhaps reminiscent of the supernatural cloud in "Young Goodman Brown," is like it a foreshadowing. In the case of Blithedale, the river has its special significance.

The next morning Coverdale finds himself seriously ill (Chapter VI, "Coverdale's Sick-Chamber"). The cold of Blithedale and the implications of Blithedale are too much for him, and he longs for his "pleasant bachelor-parlor, sunny and shadowy, curtained and carpeted." During his sickness he is nursed devotedly by Hollingsworth, whose warmth and vitality are strong supports. Coverdale recalls, "There never was any blaze of a fireside that warmed and cheered me, in the down-sinkings and shiverings of my spirit, so effectually as did the light out of those eyes, which lay so deep and dark under his shaggy brows." Hollingsworth's light, however, is firelight, not sunlight, and his virtues come from the earth and the regions below it, never from the skies. Zenobia's vitality is also present, but there is something about it that is unnatural, excessive, premature. Her ever present flower is "of the tropics, such as appeared to have sprung passionately out of a soil, the very weeds of which would be fervid and spicy." To Coverdale's morbid sensibility it becomes an obsession. "In the height of my illness, as I well recollect, I went so far as to pronounce it preternatural." Zenobia herself is a "perfectly developed rose," with "no folded petal, no latent dew-drop" in it. Looking into her eyes to discover her mystery, he sees only " 'the face of a sprite, laughing at me from the bottom of a deep well.' "

Priscilla, on the other hand, is " 'the very picture of the New England spring, subdued in tint, and rather cool, but with a capacity of sunshine, and bringing us a few alpine blossoms, as earnest of something richer, though hardly more beautiful, hereafter. The best type of her,' " concludes Coverdale, " 'is one of those anemones' " (Chapter VIII, "A Modern Arcadia"). The more skeptical Zenobia remarks about Priscilla's future prospects that girls like Priscilla " 'are all alike, while on the sunny side of experience.' " The narrator himself finds that his illness has been no less than a death and a rebirth, as he once more enters into sunlight:

> No otherwise could I have rid myself of a thousand follies, fripperies, prejudices, habits, and other such worldly dust as inevitably settles upon the crowd along the broad highway, giving them all one sordid aspect, before noontime, however freshly they may have begun their pilgrimage, in the dewy morning.

The earth itself seems rejuvenated, the Blithedale experiment most hopeful. "Emerging into the genial sunshine, I half fancied that the labors of the brotherhood had already realized some of Fourier's predictions." Age, "incrusted over with a stony layer of habits," is too opaque for the light of Blithedale to penetrate, and "youth, too, in its early dawn, was hardly more adapted to our purpose;

for it would behold the morning radiance of its own spirit beaming over the very same spots of withered grass and barren sand, whence most of us had seen it vanish." For the true stalwarts of the community, however, the realities of Blithedale are salutary. Recalls Coverdale, "After a reasonable training, the yeoman-life throve well with us. Our faces took the sunburn kindly. . . ."

Hollingsworth, the man of fire and darkness, is not all genial warmth and kindness. Looking too high, he is in danger of turning "godlike benevolence" into "all-devouring egotism" (Chapter IX, "Hollingsworth, Zenobia, Priscilla"). To Coverdale, considering him in solitude, he sometimes seems a fiend from the Pit:

> In my recollection of his dark and impressive countenance, the features grew more sternly prominent than the reality, duskier in their depth and shadow, and more lurid in their light; the frown, that had merely flitted across his brow, seemed to have contorted it with an adamantine wrinkle.

This, Coverdale admits, may be a morbid fancy: "On meeting him again, I was often filled with remorse, when his deep eyes beamed kindly upon me, as with the glow of a household fire that was burning in a cave." Still, however, the fancy recurs: "In my wood-walks, and in my silent chamber, the dark face frowned at me again."

In the safety of Blithedale, Priscilla has "now grown to be a very pretty girl" and still keeps "budding and blossoming." In this Arcadia she has become gay and playful. The author comments:

> Girls are incomparably wilder and more effervescent than boys, more untamable, and regardless of rule and limit, with

an ever-shifting variety, breaking continually into new modes of fun, yet with a harmonious propriety through all. Their steps, their voices, appear free as the wind, but keep consonance with a strain of music inaudible to us.

Such is Priscilla, growing with the freedom and harmony of nature itself, "as if we could see Nature shaping out a woman before our very eyes, and yet had only a more reverential sense of the mystery of a woman's soul and frame." To the watching Coverdale she is too free, too regardless of the darker side of things. She seems to him "like a butterfly, at play in a flickering bit of sunshine, and mistaking it for a broad and eternal summer."

One day in July a visitor appears from Boston, the shadowy Mr. Moodie. "Appears" is perhaps an ill-chosen word, since he objects to being seen and has "a queer appearance of hiding himself behind the patch on his left eye." Coverdale,

> making my prey of people's individualities, as my custom was . . . tried to identify my mind with the old fellow's, and take his view of the world, as if looking through a smoke-blackened glass at the sun. It robbed the landscape of all its life.

Mr. Hooper must have had somewhat the same view of the world from behind his black veil, and indeed the two men's names have a vague resemblance. The aforesaid landscape, as it happens, is rich, vital, and beautiful, with the variety and modulation that characterizes the Romantic picturesque:

> Those pleasantly swelling slopes of our farm, descending towards the wide meadows, through which sluggishly circled

the brimfull tide of the Charles, bathing the long sedges on its hither and farther shores; the broad, sunny gleam over the winding water; that peculiar picturesqueness of the scene, where capes and headlands put themselves boldly forth upon the perfect level of the meadow, as into a green lake, with inlets between the promontories; the shadowy woodland, with twinkling showers of light falling into its depths; the sultry heat vapor, which rose everywhere like incense, and in which my soul delighted, as indicating so rich a fervor in the passionate day, and in the earth that was burning with its love—I beheld all these things as through old Moodie's eyes.

Seldom is Hawthorne so romantic, so outgoing in his approach to nature. Probably it involves the contrast, and another plane of vision. First, the vision of old Moodie is superimposed upon it; next, the duskiness of Coverdale's own retrospective point of view; and finally, his grim reflection: "When my eyes are dimmer than they have yet come to be, I will go thither again, and see if I did not catch the tone of his mind aright, and if the cold and lifeless tint of his perceptions be not then repeated in my own."

To old Moodie it is a wonder that his "pale little girl" Priscilla has "a bloom in her cheeks." Hollingsworth thinks the old man cannot be in his right mind; it does not strike Coverdale, however, "that our strange guest was really beside himself, but only that his mind needed screwing up, like an instrument long out of tune, the strings of which have ceased to vibrate smartly and sharply." Besides, the old man might have his uses at Blithedale:

> Methought it would be profitable for us, projectors of a happy life, to welcome this old gray shadow, and cherish

him as one of us, let him creep about our domain, in order that he might be a little merrier for our sakes, and we, sometimes, a little sadder for his. Human destinies look ominous, without some perceptible intermixture of the sable or the gray.

Coverdale himself, we find, is not able to bear too long a spell of unrelieved sunshine. Not long after, in fact (Chapter XI, "The Wood-Path"), he seeks "the deepest wood-seclusion that lay anywhere around us." Blithedale is relatively remote from the world, but

> Unless renewed by a yet farther withdrawal towards the inner circle of self-communion, I lost the better part of my individuality. My thoughts became of little worth, and my sensibilities grew as arid as a tuft of moss (a thing whose life is in the shade, the rain, or the noontide dew), crumbling in the sunshine after long expectance of a shower.

On this particular occasion Coverdale is not destined to attain his wishes. Instead, like Young Goodman Brown on a similar excursion, he encounters a rather sinister stranger, whom, unlike Goodman Brown, he does not expect.

This man, though "as handsome a man as ever I beheld," is somehow false and jarring. His face has "an indecorum in it; . . . in his eyes (although they might have artifice enough of another sort)" there is "the naked exposure of something that ought not to be left prominent." The stranger, Westervelt, is at once black and bright, perversely vital. "His hair, as well as his beard and moustache," is "coal-black"; his eyes, too, are "black and sparkling, and his teeth remarkably brilliant." (We learn presently that his teeth are false.) He wears a gold chain, "exquisitely wrought, across his vest." Like Judge Pyncheon's, his linen is impeccable, almost shockingly white. He wears a pin that reminds us of Zenobia's exotic flower; it is set with a gem that glimmers, "in the leafy shadow" where he stands, "like a living tip of fire." And, like the devil in "Young Goodman Brown," he carries "a stick with a wooden head, carved in vivid imitation of that of a serpent."

Coverdale reports that in conversation Westervelt's "black eyes sparkled at me, whether with fun or malice I knew not, but certainly as if the Devil were peeping out of them." Entertainingly, Westervelt's view of Hollingsworth has a diabolic tinge; he has heard of the latter as "a brawny, shaggy, grim, and ill-favored personage." Westervelt has a "metallic laugh," and he is so pleased by his own sketch of Hollingsworth's character and looks that "in the excess of his delight" he opens his mouth wide and discloses "a gold band around the upper part of his teeth; thereby making it apparent that every one of his brilliant grinders and incisors" is "a sham." Laughter itself is in Hawthorne ordinarily inharmonious, and between Westervelt's laughter and his incongruities Coverdale himself unwillingly bursts out laughing:

> I felt as if the whole man were a moral and physical humbug; his wonderful beauty of face, for aught I knew, might be removeable like a mask; and, tall and comely as his figure looked, he was perhaps but a wizened little elf, gray and decrepit, with nothing genuine about him, save the wicked expression of his grin. The fantasy of his spectral character so wrought upon me, together with the contagion of his

strange mirth on my sympathies, that I soon began to laugh as loudly as himself.

For Coverdale, his amusement is a defeat, since he has permitted himself to yield to the spiritual aura of his interlocutor.

A little later Coverdale is more successful in finding seclusion, in a favorite spot of his, a "kind of leafy cave, high upward into the air, among the midmost branches of a white-pine tree" (Chapter XII, "Coverdale's Hermitage"). "This hermitage," he says, "was my one exclusive possession, while I counted myself a brother of the socialists. It symbolized my individuality, and aided me in keeping it inviolate." From here, invisible himself, he looks out upon Blithedale and its inhabitants, meditating upon their interrelations. His heart goes out to Priscilla, to whom he sends "a message by a passing bird," as it flies onward "into the sunny atmosphere." He warns her silently that " 'Hollingsworth's heart is on fire with his own purpose, but icy for all human affection' " and that, " 'if any mortal really cares for her, it is myself, and not even I, for her realities ... but for the fancy-work with which I have idly decked her out!' " The qualification, characteristic of his intense tortuous self-consciousness, has run through all his views of the puzzling Priscilla.

For whatever reason, he finds himself in a "mood of disbelief" of things in general. Perhaps it is the effect of the sun and nature, vital but less subtly harmonious than earlier in the day:

The pleasant scent of the wood, evolved by the hot sun, stole up to my nostrils, as if I had been an idol in its niche.

Many trees mingled their fragrance into a thousand-fold odor. Possibly, there was a sensual influence in the broad light of noon that lay beneath me.

Hearing somewhere beneath him the sound of Westervelt's laugh, however, he recognizes,

as chiefly due to this man's influence, the sceptical and sneering view which, just now, had filled my mental vision in regard to all life's better purposes. And it was through his eyes, more than my own, that I was looking at Hollingsworth, with his glorious, if impracticable dream, and at the noble earthliness of Zenobia's character, and even at Priscilla, whose impalpable grace lay so singularly between disease and beauty. The essential charm of each had vanished.

Coverdale's excess of sympathy, it might be said, ends by diffusion in a failure of sympathy and belief. It is not long since he has been looking through the eyes of old Moodie and yet simultaneously seeing with his own. Meanwhile, he finds himself an involuntary eavesdropper at an interview between Zenobia and Westervelt, in which it is clear that despite her strength and her unwillingness she is being forced into serving some purpose of his. In her emotion Coverdale recalls,

Zenobia had a rich, though varying color. It was, most of the while, a flame, and anon a sudden paleness. Her eyes glowed, so that their light sometimes flashed upward to me, as when the sun throws a dazzle from some bright object on the ground.

Her passionate intensity avails her nothing, however, against Westervelt, who is impervious in his cold skepticism to both light and heat: ". . . he was not a whit more warmed by Zenobia's passion, than a salamander by the heat of its native furnace."

The interpolated story of "Zenobia's Legend" (Chapter XIII), which obliquely retells the story of Priscilla's career as the Veiled Lady and reveals the purpose of Westervelt's visit, also hits at Coverdale's failure in belief. Like Theodore in the story, he will not risk his chances and take on faith the being that the mysterious veil covers. The Lady, or Zenobia as narrator, puts the case directly to him:

> "Has not thy heart recognized me? Dost thou come hither, not in holy faith, nor with a pure and generous purpose, but in scornful scepticism and idle curiosity? Still, thou mayst lift the veil! But from that instant, Theodore, I am doomed to be thy evil fate; nor wilt thou ever taste another breath of happiness!"

The comparison is unduly hard on Coverdale, and Zenobia, who has just abandoned Priscilla to Westervelt, is no fit person to make it. Nevertheless, the Lady's doom is carried out in the end. Priscilla is of course also the innocent cause of the destruction of Zenobia herself, the narrator of the tale.

The next two chapters move quietly toward the crisis that finally forces Coverdale to leave the community of Blithedale. Chapter XIV, "Eliot's Pulpit," has for its background a pleasant Sunday, quiet and harmonious. The brethren have gone to rest:

> Some betook themselves into the wide, dusky barn, and lay there, for hours together, on the odorous hay; while the sunstreaks and the shadows strove together—these to make the barn solemn, those to make it cheerful—and both were

conquerors; and the swallows twittered a cheery anthem, flashing into sight, or vanishing, as they darted to-and-fro among the golden rules of sunshine.

The great rock called Eliot's pulpit is also propitiously placed, amid aftergrowths which "run into an entanglement of softer wildness, among the rustling leaves of which the sun can scatter cheerfulness, as it never could among the dark-browed pines." The summit of the rock is "overshadowed by the canopy of a birch-tree," and beneath this shade, says Coverdale, "I used to see the holy Apostle of the Indians, with the sunlight flickering down upon him through the leaves, and glorifying his figure as with the half-perceptible glow of a transfiguration."

This benediction of light and shadow changes, however, as Coverdale, Zenobia, Hollingsworth, and Priscilla return through the woods from the pulpit. A compact has been made between Hollingsworth and Zenobia, and Zenobia is for the time triumphant, though far from tranquil: ". . . as the declining sun threw Zenobia's magnified shadow along the path, I beheld it tremulous; and the delicate stem of the flower, which she wore in her hair, was likewise responsive to her agitation." Priscilla senses that she has been abandoned. Her reality almost physically dwindles away: ". . . the life seemed to pass out of her, and even the substance of her figure to grow thin and gray. I almost imagined her a shadow, fading gradually into the dimness of the wood." The scene ends in a tableau, in which, "arriving nearly at the farm-house, I looked back over the long slope of pasture-land, and beheld them standing together, in the light of sunset, just on the spot where, according to the gossip of the Community, they meant to build their cottage. Priscilla, alone and forgotten, was lingering in the shadow of the wood."

As summer wears on, Hollingsworth forces Coverdale to take a stand on the great scheme for reclaiming criminals that is Hollingsworth's ruling purpose in life. Coverdale refuses to join him, though with great difficulty (Chapter XV, "A Crisis"):

> It is a mystery to me, how I withstood it. But, in truth, I saw in his scheme of philanthropy nothing but what was odious. A loathsomeness that was to be forever in my daily work! A great, black ugliness of sin, which he proposed to collect out of a thousand human hearts, and that we should spend our lives in an experiment of transmuting it into virtue!

Soon afterward Coverdale leaves Blithedale for a while, temporarily disenchanted:

> Blithedale was no longer what it had been. Everything was suddenly faded. The sun-burnt and arid aspect of our woods and pastures, beneath the August sky, did but imperfectly symbolize the lack of dew and moisture that, since yesterday, as it were, had blighted my fields of thought, and penetrated to the innermost and shadiest of my contemplative recesses.

His feelings have changed, though the scene remains the same (Chapter XVI, "Leave-Takings"):

> The change will be recognized by many, who, after a period of happiness, have endeavored to go on with the same kind of life, in the same scene, in spite of the alteration or withdrawal of some principal circumstance. They discover (what heretofore, perhaps, they had not known) that it was this which gave the bright color and vivid reality to the whole affair.

Returning to Boston, Coverdale puts up at a hotel, where he is forced to content himself with "a back-room of the third story" (Chapter XVII, "The Hotel"). As in the house of the seven gables when Phoebe is away, all is changed for the worse; the sun has departed:

> The day was lowering, with occasional gusts of rain, and an ugly-tempered east-wind, which seemed to come right off the chill and melancholy sea, hardly mitigated by sweeping over the roofs, and amalgamating itself with the dusky element of city-smoke.

Blithedale and its influences have vanished:

> All the effeminacy of past days had returned upon me at once. Summer as it still was, I ordered a coal-fire in the rusty grate, and was glad to find myself growing a little too warm with an artificial temperature.

To Coverdale, disjoined from relationships, all is unreal; he is suspended between different worlds:

> At one moment, the very circumstances now surrounding me—my coal-fire, and the dingy room in the bustling hotel—appeared far off and intangible. The next instant, Blithedale looked vague, as if it were at a distance both in time and space, and so shadowy, that a question might be raised whether the whole affair had been anything more than the thoughts of a speculative man. I had never before experienced a mood that so robbed the actual world of its solidity.

Yet the mood has its charm, "on which—a devoted epicure of my own emotions—I resolved to pause, and enjoy the moral sillabub until quite dissolved away." Outside his windows is the life and movement of the city, "just as valuable, in its way, as the sighing of the breeze among the birch-trees, that overshadowed Eliot's pulpit." Yet he is uncertain "about plunging into this muddy tide of human activity and pastime."

Coverdale looks out of his windows, as from the vantage point of his "hermitage" at Blithedale, a spectator of life. What he sees is a "little portion of the backside of the universe," in the frame of a "gray sky, the weathercock of a steeple" that rises in the distance, and "a sprinkle of small, spiteful-looking raindrops on the window-pane." The view is uninspiring. Nevertheless,

> . . . there is far more of the picturesque, more truth to native and characteristic tendencies, and vastly greater suggestiveness, in the back view of a residence, whether in town or country, than in its front. The latter is always artificial; it is meant for the world's eye, and is therefore a veil and a concealment. Realities keep in the rear, and put forward an advance-guard of show and humbug.

Before the watcher, in a "row of fashionable dwellings," is "a rather stylish boarding-house," which particularly draws his attention. On the peak of one of its dormer windows sits a lone dove,

> looking very dreary and forlorn. . . . All at once, this dove spread her wings, and launching herself in the air, came flying so straight across the intervening space, that I fully expected her to alight directly on my window-sill. In the latter part of her course, however, she swerved aside, flew upward, and vanished, as did likewise the slight, fantastic pathos with which I had invested her.

The dove, however, is a symbol of Priscilla, and her swerve away from the window is the pattern of her relation to Coverdale. Cautiously reaching out to her, he never quite attracts her to him.

The next day, on "a gray and dripping forenoon," he takes his place at the window once more. His mood still unsettled, he thinks "how the gusty rain was drifting over the slopes and valleys of our farm; how wet must be the foliage that overshadowed the pulpit-rock; how cheerless, in such a day, my hermitage. . . . I had wrenched myself too suddenly out of an accustomed sphere." He suffers, too, from "idle and shapeless regrets." He has abandoned his friends to their fate. "That cold tendency, between instinct and intellect, which made me pry with a speculative interest into people's passions and impulses, appeared to have gone far towards unhumanizing my heart." Yet in retrospect the narrator reflects, as is his regular pattern, that his self-blame is beside the mark:

> A man cannot always decide for himself whether his own heart is cold or warm. It now impresses me, that, if I erred at all, in regard to Hollingsworth, Zenobia, and Priscilla, it was through too much sympathy, rather than too little.

Nor has he separated himself from his friends, for as he watches the windows of the house opposite (Chapter XVIII, "The Boarding-House"), they appear, half-veiled as it were by festooned curtains and only gradually revealing their identities—first Priscilla, dimly visible; then Zenobia, more distinct; finally and significantly Westervelt, in place of Hollingsworth. "There now needed only Hollingsworth and old Moodie to complete the knot of characters." Their presence, however, would not fit the situation. Westervelt, with his "cat-like circumspection," catches sight of the watching Coverdale and summons Zenobia, who definitively shuts off his view "by letting down a white linen curtain between the festoons of the damask ones." It falls "like the drop-curtain of a theatre, in the interval between the acts." Priscilla has also disappeared from the window of her separate room in the house. But the dove keeps "her desolate perch, on the peak of the attic-window," still tacitly asking to be rescued.

After the interval there is more light, shading off into darkness again. Chapter XIX, "Zenobia's Drawing-Room," is full of halftones, shadings, and varying effects, which reflect incomplete but suggestive aspects of reality. As the day passes, Coverdale sits "in my rocking-chair, too far withdrawn from the window to expose myself to another rebuke, like that already inflicted." The wind shifts, and the view changes:

> Late in the afternoon, the weathercock on the church-spire indicated a change of wind; the sun shone dimly out, as if the golden wine of its beams were mingled half-and-half with water. Nevertheless, they kindled up the whole range of edifices, threw a glow over the windows, glistened on the wet roofs, and, slowly withdrawing upward, perched upon the chimney-tops; thence they took a higher flight, and lingered an instant on the tip of the spire, making it the final point of more cheerful light in the whole sombre scene. The next moment, it was all gone.

The sunlight is in its very dimness a momentary benediction and a sacrament. The scene to be played, however, is variously and artificially lighted. First, at a distance, it is a shadow play:

When I returned to my chamber, the glow of an astral lamp was penetrating mistily through the white curtain of Zenobia's drawing-room. The shadow of a passing figure was now-and-then cast upon this medium, but with too vague an outline for even my adventurous conjectures to read the hieroglyphic that it presented.

Coverdale, taking courage, leaves his room and presents himself boldly at Zenobia's door. When it is opened, the light in her chambers is unnaturally brilliant. A "bright illumination" streams through the door of the front drawing room, and Coverdale has scarcely stepped across the threshold when Zenobia comes forward to meet him, "laughing, and with an extended hand." The atmosphere is theatrical, as if all were arranged to foster an artful illusion for a pleased but baffled spectator. Coverdale senses the distance that now separates him from his hostess:

How great was the contrast betwixt this interview and our first meeting. Then, in the warm light of the country fireside, Zenobia had greeted me cheerily and hopefully, with a full sisterly grasp of the hand.

The difference is between nature and contrived art,

as complete as between her appearance, at that time—so simply attired, and with only the one superb flower in her hair—and now, when her beauty set off by all that dress and ornament could do for it.

Zenobia is indeed all light, a cynosure. Her clothes and the "flaming jewels on her neck" serve as "lamps to display the personal advantages" which require "nothing less than such an illumination, to be fully seen." Even her invariable flower has "undergone a cold and bright transfiguration";

it is "a flower exquisitely imitated in jeweller's work, and imparting the last touch" that transforms Zenobia "into a work of art."

There is a concentration of light, in fact, which seems calculated on the one hand to glorify Zenobia, a revelation of a deity in her temple, and on the other to confuse and overpower the onlooker:

> Her manner bewildered me. Literally, moreover, I was dazzled by the brilliancy of the room. A chandelier hung down in the centre, glowing with I know not how many lights; there were separate lamps, also, on two or three tables, and on marble brackets, adding their white radiance to that of the chandelier.

The whole is "repeated and doubled by the reflection of a great mirror," which shows him "Zenobia's proud figure, likewise, and my own." The double-visioned Coverdale, himself mirror-like in his continual shifts between the inward and the outward view, perceives in himself "a positive effort to bear up against the effect" Zenobia seeks to produce. He reasons against her, "in my secret mind," and strives so to keep his "footing." Thus ironically he cannot achieve full faith in Zenobia as he fails in full faith in Priscilla, like Theodore in his skepticism of the illusion of the Veiled Lady.

Zenobia is, however, too powerful for all his "opposing struggles." Some basic reality in her persists through all the dazzlement of lighting, though its nature remains ambiguous:

> I hardly know whether I then beheld Zenobia in her truest attitude, or whether that were the truer one in which she

had presented herself at Blithedale. In both, there was something like the illusion which a great actress flings around her.

Irritated, Coverdale tries to penetrate the illusion: "She should be compelled to give me a glimpse of something true; some nature, some passion, no matter whether right or wrong, provided it were real." He succeeds, by making a scornful allusion to the absent Hollingsworth, whereupon

> Zenobia's eyes darted lightning; her cheeks flushed; the vividness of her expression was like the effect of a powerful light, flaming up suddenly within her. My experiment had fully succeeded. She had shown me the true flesh and blood of her heart. . . .

Still skillfully baiting her, Coverdale suggests that Hollingsworth may be falling in love with the pliant Priscilla. Zenobia has turned aside. But Coverdale glimpses the reflection of her face in the mirror and sees that it is "very pale;—as pale, in her rich attire, as if a shroud were round her." Here, considering the blaze of light that has surrounded her, one may anticipate the fact that Zenobia will die invisible beneath the blackness of midnight, through the joint agency of Hollingsworth and Priscilla.

Yet, as though to deny the foreshadowing, Priscilla now appears at Zenobia's summons, a mere "leaf, floating on the dark current of events, without influencing them by her own choice or plan" (Chapter XX, "They Vanish"). Her sort of beauty is shadowy, "not positive and material enough to bear up against a mistaken choice of color, for instance, or fashion." She is at once less vivid than Zenobia and more natural and harmonious. At present Priscilla is dressed in garments that significantly suggest the Veiled Lady: "pure white, set off with some kind of a gauzy fabric, which—as I bring up her figure in my memory, with a faint gleam on her shadowy hair, and her dark eyes bent shyly on mine, through all the vanished years—seems to be floating about her like a mist."

Coverdale asks himself "what Zenobia meant by evolving so much loveliness out of this poor girl." Several answers are conceivable, whatever Zenobia's precise intention. For one, pictorially Priscilla adds to the artistic illusion of the scene, blending with its other elements. In a slightly different perspective, she figures to the imagination a synthesis that can never literally occur: "the sheen and splendor of Zenobia's presence" takes "nothing from Priscilla's softer spell, if it might not rather be thought to add to it." Conversely, if Zenobia appears as a goddess, Priscilla is then perhaps a victim decked out for the sacrifice, and powerless. " 'I am blown about like a leaf,' " she tells Coverdale. " 'I never have any free-will.' " Last among the characters in this scene, Westervelt at length makes his entrance, "elaborately dressed, as if for some grand entertainment." As before, he himself seems an illusion, who despite his "personal beauty" and "polish of manner" gives Coverdale "a creeping of the flesh, as when, feeling about in a dark place, one touches something cold and slimy." As a master of illusion, it is highly appropriate for him to be present in this contrived and illusory scene, and even more so since he has come to take Priscilla to her public performance in the illusion of the Veiled Lady, though Coverdale does not know it.

In the hope of further enlightenment Coverdale seeks

out old Moodie, whom he finds in a saloon (Chapter XXI, "An Old Acquaintance"). Characteristically, the old man is hard to see when Coverdale finds him:

> I had begun to despair of meeting old Moodie, when, all at once, I recognized his hand and arm, protruding from behind a screen that was set up for the accommodation of bashful topers. . . . His existence looked so colorless and torpid—so very faintly shadowed on the canvass of reality— that I was half afraid lest he should altogether disappear, even while my eyes were fixed full upon his figure. He was certainly the wretchedest old ghost in the world. . . .

Coverdale guesses that wine may make him more accessible:

> There was one method, however, of bringing him out into somewhat stronger relief. . . . Nor could I think it a matter for the recording angel to write down against me, if—with my painful consciouness of the frost in this old man's blood, and the positive ice that had congealed about his heart—I should thaw him out, were it only for an hour, with the summer warmth of a little wine.

This substitute for sunshine is effective; instead of resembling "a gray kennel-rat," Moodie begins "to take the aspect of a decayed gentleman," and even his clothes look less shabby, while he displays "a certain exuberance and elaborateness of gesture, and manner, oddly in contrast with all that I had hitherto seen of him." And he talks freely.

Moodie has been Fauntleroy, "a man of wealth, and magnificent tastes, and prodigal expenditure" (Chapter XXII, "Fauntleroy"), whose life was centered in outward show. "His whole being seemed to have crystallized itself into an external splendor, wherewith he glittered in the eyes of the world, and had no other life than upon this gaudy surface." Zenobia, his daughter by his first wife, is the child of his splendor, "whom he took from the beneficent hand of God with no just sense of her immortal value, but as a man, already rich in gems, would receive another jewel. If he loved her, it was because she shone." After a few years of "corruscating continually an unnatural light" he lost his gold, without which he was nothing, and in trying to recoup made himself liable to criminal prosecution. "He saw himself in imminent peril of losing all that had hitherto distinguished him; and, conscious of no innate worth to fall back upon, he recoiled from this calamity, with the instinct of a soul shrinking from annihilation." Fauntleroy escaped criminal trial, but he was ruined and was quickly forgotten even by "his closest former intimates. . . . The man had laid no real touch on any mortal's heart. Being a mere image, an optical delusion, created by the sunshine of prosperity, it was his law to vanish into the shadow of the first intervening cloud."

Fauntleroy, the man of show and glitter, now hid himself away:

Instead of any longer seeking to live in the sight of the world, his impulse was to shrink into the nearest obscurity, and to be unseen of men, were it possible, even while standing before their eyes. . . . Hardly, it was averred, within the memory of those who knew him now, had he the hardihood to show his full front to the world. He skulked in corners, and crept about in a sort of noonday twilight, making himself gray and misty, at all hours, with his morbid intolerance of sunshine.

In his wretchedness and obscurity Fauntleroy took a second wife, "a forlorn, meek-spirited, feeble young woman," a "poor phantom" by whom he had another daughter, Priscilla. He sometimes wondered

whether the grandee of yesterday or the pauper of to-day were real. But, in my [Coverdale's] mind, the one and the other were alike impalpable. In truth, it was Fauntleroy's fatality to behold whatever he touched dissolve. After a few years, his second wife (dim shadow that she had always been) faded finally out of the world, and left Fauntleroy to deal as he might with their pale and nervous child.

The child Priscilla was also shadowy: "There was a lack of human substance in her; it seemed as if, were she to stand up in a sunbeam, it would pass right through her figure, and trace out the cracked and dusty window-panes upon the naked floor." But she could love, and her father told her stories of his former prosperity, and especially of her beautiful sister. "And, out of the loneliness of her sad little existence, Priscilla's love grew, and tended upward, and twined itself perseveringly around this unseen sister; as a grape-vine might strive to clamber out of a gloomy hollow among the rocks, and embrace a young tree, standing in the sunny warmth above." The child's dimness was strangely mingled with light, her weakness with strength:

They called her ghost-child, and said that she could indeed vanish, when she pleased, but could never, in her densest moments, make herself quite visible. The sun, at mid-day, would shine through her; in the first gray of the twilight, she lost all the distinctness of her outline; and, if you followed the dim thing into a dark corner, behold! she was not there.

Yet Priscilla had strange, almost supernatural gifts:

> Never stirring out of the dusky house, she sometimes talked
> of distant places and splendid rooms, as if she had just left
> them. Hidden things were visible to her . . . and silence was
> audible. And, in all the world, there was nothing so difficult
> to be endured, by those who had any dark secret to conceal,
> as the glance of Priscilla's timid and melancholy eyes.

Thus she was a touchstone of truth and a test of faith and
imagination—a test that was failed by others at their peril.

Priscilla's gifts as a medium have at length put her in the
power of the shrewd charlatan Westervelt; and it is an
interesting complexity that as the Veiled Lady her true
gifts further an imposture, that her veil of illusion is the
symbol of her truth. Zenobia is of course her opposite.
Summoned by Fauntleroy-Moodie, who is unknown to
her, Zenobia shines forth, the child of his grandeur.

> Moodie took the one lamp that showed the discomfort and
> sordidness of his abode, and approaching Zenobia, held it
> up, so as to gain the more perfect view of her, from top to
> toe. So obscure was the chamber, that you could see the
> reflection of her diamonds thrown upon the dingy wall,
> and flickering with the rise and fall of Zenobia's breath. It
> was the splendor of those jewels on her neck, like lamps that
> burn before some fair temple, and the jewelled flower in
> her hair, more than the murky yellow light, that helped him
> to see her beauty.

Proud of her, he leaves her with the wealth that is legally
his, an inheritance from his brother: " 'Zenobia has the
splendor, and not the shame. Let the world admire her,
and be dazzled by her, the brilliant child of my prosperity!

It is Fauntleroy that still shines through her!' " Yet on the same night of this interview, as it happens, Priscilla, a "poor, pallid flower," is "either snatched from Zenobia's hand, or flung wilfully away."

In Chapter XXIII, "A Village-Hall," Priscilla makes her last appearance as the Veiled Lady, several weeks after Coverdale's meeting with old Moodie. Coverdale, fittingly enough for the events of the chapter, has brooded about the incidents and the characters whom he has watched over, "rendering them more misty and unsubstantial than at first, by the quantity of speculative musing, thus kneaded in with them." He and Hollingsworth are both in the audience when the Veiled Lady takes the stage. She is "enveloped in a long veil of silvery whiteness." It falls about her, "like the texture of a summer cloud, with a kind of vagueness, so that the outline of the form, beneath it," cannot be "accurately discerned." Westervelt, a "dark, earthly magician," tells the audience, " 'That silvery veil is, in one sense, an enchantment, having been dipt, as it were, and essentially imbued, through the potency of my art, with the fluid medium of spirits. Slight and ethereal as it seems, the limitations of time and space have no existence within its folds.' " He intends a lie and yet speaks the truth. The veil has preserved as well as isolated Priscilla:

> Within that encircling veil, though an evil hand had flung it over her, there was as deep a seclusion as if this forsaken girl had, all the while, been sitting under the shadow of Eliot's pulpit, in the Blithedale woods, at the feet of him who now summoned her to the shelter of his arms. . . . she fled to Hollingsworth, like one escaping from her deadliest enemy, and was safe forever.

Two days later Coverdale sets out again for Blithedale (Chapter XXIV, "The Masqueraders"). It is a lovely day in early autumn:

> The pathway of that walk still runs along, with sunny freshness, through my memory. I know not why it should be so. But my mental eye can even now discern the September grass, bordering the pleasant roadside with a brighter verdure than while the summer-heats were scorching it; the trees, too, mostly green, although, here and there, a branch or shrub has donned its vesture of crimson and gold. . . . I see the tufted barberry bushes, with their small clusters of scarlet fruit; the toadstools, likewise, some spotlessly white, others yellow or red—mysterious growths, springing suddenly from no root or seed, and growing nobody can tell why or wherefore. In this respect, they resembled many of the emotions in my breast.

Coverdale's momentary happiness is unaccountable, save as the one last freedom that the story permits him; correspondingly, it presents a patch of brightness to contrast with the darkness that follows. He quickly returns to obsessive thoughts of Zenobia, Hollingsworth, and Priscilla: ". . . still, at every turn of my shifting fantasies, the thought stared me in the face, that some evil thing had befallen us, or was ready to fall." Characteristically, he approaches Blithedale indirectly: "I would go wandering about the outskirts of the farm, and, perhaps catching sight of a solitary acquaintance, would approach him amid the brown shadows of the trees (a kind of medium fit for spirits departed and revisitant, like myself), and entreat him to tell me how all things were." He walks "by the dark, sluggish river" and remembers pausing on the bank, above one of its blackest and most placid pools—(the very spot, with the barkless stump of a tree aslantwise over the water, is depicting itself to my fancy, at this instant)—and wondering how deep it was, and if any over-laden soul had ever flung its weight of mortality in thither, and if it thus escaped the burthen, or only made it heavier.

The masquerade he presently encounters adds confusion to his homecoming, "a concourse of strange figures beneath the overshadowing branches." They appear, vanish, and reappear, "confusedly, with the streaks of sunlight glimmering down upon them."

Chapter XXV, "The Three Together," recounts Zenobia's defeat and Hollingsworth's condemnation of her. In her vigorous counterattack she regrets the want of " 'a little kinder smile of Him who sent me hither.' " As for Hollingsworth, " 'blackest of your sins, you stifled down your inmost consciousness!—you did a deadly wrong to your own heart!' " Alone with the pitying Coverdale (Chapter XXVI, "Zenobia and Coverdale"), she reasserts her superiority to Priscilla:

> "After all, he has flung away what would have served him better than the poor, pale flower he kept. . . . For will he never, in many an hour of darkness, need that proud intellectual sympathy which he might have had from me?—the sympathy that would flash light along his course, and guide as well as cheer him?"

Blithedale, she says, has been " 'a foolish dream! Yet it gave us some pleasant summer days, and bright hopes, while they lasted.' " Now she will " 'become a Catholic, for the sake of going into a nunnery. When you next hear of Zenobia, her face will be behind the black-veil; so look your last at it now—for all is over!' "

Coverdale lingers at the base of Eliot's pulpit:

> The sunshine withdrew up the tree-trunks, and flickered on the topmost boughs; gray twilight made the wood obscure; the stars brightened out; the pendent boughs became wet with chill autumnal dews. But I was listless, worn-out with emotion on my own behalf, and sympathy for others, and had no heart to leave my comfortless lair, beneath the rock.

He dreams, and awakes with "the risen moon shining upon the rugged face of the rock, and myself all in a tremble." Zenobia, he has reason to think, has indeed sought the shelter of the black veil.

After summoning Hollingsworth and Silas Foster from the community, he hastens with them "to the particular spot, on the river-bank, which I had paused to contemplate, in the course of my afternoon's ramble" (Chapter XXVII, "Midnight"). Here he has found Zenobia's handkerchief. The moon is up, but no moonlight seems to fall on the river itself, which moves "imperceptibly away, a broad, black, inscrutable depth, keeping its own secrets from the eye of man, as impenetrably as mid-ocean could." The searchers probe the pool where to judge from the current a body would probably be lodged:

> So obscure, however, so awfully mysterious, was that dark stream, that . . . I might as well have tried to look into the enigma of the eternal world, to discover what had become of Zenobia's soul, as into the river's depths, to find her body.

Thus the bright Zenobia lies in total darkness at the last.

To the materialist Westervelt her case is " 'twenty years of a brilliant lifetime thrown away for a mere woman's whim!' " Priscilla last appears with "a veiled happiness in her fair and quiet countenance." As for Coverdale, in his final "Confession" (Chapter XXIX) he speaks of the "years that are darkening around me"; of "our beautiful scheme of a noble and unselfish life, and how fair, in that first summer, appeared the prospect that it might endure for generations"; and finally of his love for Priscilla, which "will throw a gleam of light over my behavior throughout the foregoing incidents." But Priscilla herself has never shone upon him, nor perhaps would he ever have accepted the light that he has finally recognized within her.

V. THE MARBLE FAUN

ONATELLO the faun
and the saintly Hilda are the sunshine characters of *The
Marble Faun*, with Miriam and her shadow, the artist's
model, representing the opposing darkness. Miriam, it
must be said, like Hester Prynne and Zenobia, bears a light
within her; and further, if she is treated as the center of
the book, Donatello and Hilda are her angels of light, and
the model is a dark angel hovering near her. In a more
Freudian interpretation, Dorothy Waples has suggested
that the other characters are simply the principal aspects
of Miriam's divided psyche.

To apply an insight applied by several critics to Hester
and Dimmesdale, Donatello's proper milieu is natural
sunshine, while Hilda's is the white light of divinity. He is
the creature of the Arcadian Golden Age; her habitat is
Eden. The distinction is not absolute, either in *The Scarlet
Letter* or in *The Marble Faun*, and in the latter novel
nature and divinity are not infrequently fused, in such
phrases as "the blessed sunshine." The lowest common
denominator that links Hilda and Donatello, however, is
their youth.

Full sunlight is not the right medium for art, as Miriam explains in her painter's studio. Its meaning depends upon focus, upon contrasts. In this regard she might well be speaking for Hawthorne's total theory of the romance. On the other hand, to Hawthorne's good Protestants the Roman Catholic church is unrighteous in interposing its gorgeous stained-glass windows between divinity and the eye of man. Yet the church has its light, and *The Marble Faun* often refers to paintings in terms of light, glory, and splendor. As a supremely gifted copyist of great art, Hilda is the conservator and even the regenerator of its light and its life. Through the sunshine of sympathy, she is able to see and grasp the vital principle of the great artworks of the past. *The Marble Faun*, indeed, contains Hawthorne's strongest and most explicit sunshine-divinity relationships: in Hilda, in sunny St. Peter's, in the statue of Pope Julius at Perugia (Chapter XXXV, "The Bronze Pontiff's Benediction"). And it may well be that his culminating image of totality is the sun-and-shadow picture of landscape and sky that Kenyon sees from the tower of Monte Beni (Chapter XXIX, "On the Battlements").

From the outset *The Marble Faun* is dissevered from "the broad and simple daylight" of America, "my dear native land" (Preface). All is to have a tinge of the picturesque and strange, the heightening that belongs to art. The book commences in "the sculpture gallery in the Capitol at Rome," where

stand the Antinous, the Amazon, the Lycian Apollo, the Juno; all famous productions of antique sculpture, and still

shining in the undiminished majesty and beauty of their ideal
life, although the marble that embodies them is yellow with
time, and perhaps corroded by the damp earth in which
they lay buried for centuries.

Perhaps the light itself is brighter in the darkness of Rome's
antiquity. From the windows of the gallery one may see
"the great sweep of the Coliseum, with the blue sky
brightening through its upper tier of arches," and further
away "the Alban Mountains, looking just the same, amid
all this decay and change, as when Romulus gazed thither-
ward over his half-finished wall." These impressions are
brought together in a hasty glance "at this bright sky, and
those blue distant mountains, and at the ruins, Etruscan,
Roman, Christian, venerable with a threefold antiquity,
and at the company of world-famous statutes in the
saloon."

This contrast of brightness and darkness is re-echoed
in a speech of Miriam's, after a sudden emotional fit that
has dismayed her companions (Chapter II, "The Faun"):
" 'Let it go as it came . . . like a thunder-shower in this
Roman sky. All is sunshine again, you see!' " And the
contrast is enforced in the following scene (Chapter III,
"Subterranean Reminiscences"), in the catacomb of St.
Calixtus, in the gloom of which occasionally "a little daylight" glimmers down, "or even a streak of sunshine" falls
into a burial niche. Characteristically, Hilda and Donatello
are repelled by the experience, the latter quite forcibly.
" 'I hate it all!' " cries Donatello, with "peculiar energy.
'Dear friends, let us hasten back into the blessed daylight!' " There is a story of a ghost who wanders this

catacomb, "a pagan of old Rome, who hid himself in order to spy out and betray the blessed saints, who then dwelt and worshipped in these dismal places." Now, as the legend tells, " 'What this lost wretch pines for, almost as much as for the blessed sunshine, is a companion to be miserable with him.' "

The superstition has its true counterpart in the dark figure of the model, who has indeed been haunting the catacomb. With some mysterious past relationship to Miriam, he now reattaches himself to her. " 'Inquire not what I am, nor wherefore I abide in the darkness,' " he says. " 'Henceforth, I am nothing but a shadow behind her footsteps. She came to me when I sought her not. She has called me forth, and must abide the consequences of my reappearance in the world' " (Chapter IV, "The Spectre of the Catacomb"). Subsequently the model's features, "or some shadow or reminiscence of them" may be discerned "in her sketches and pictures." Miriam, in a jest that is grounded in underlying truth, forebodes that, "in a few more months, she must take an eternal farewell of the sun!" The sun-loving Donatello nourishes "a singular prejudice against the mysterious, dusky, death-scented apparition." He is dismayed by "the shadow of the model, always flung into the light" which Miriam diffuses around her.

In her studio (Chapter V), Miriam asks Donatello, " '. . . why do you come into this shadowy room of mine?' " He asks, " 'Why do you make it so shadowy?' " Miriam says:

"We artists purposely exclude sunshine, and all but a partial light, . . . because we think it necessary to put ourselves at odds with Nature before trying to imitate her. That strikes you very strangely, does it not? But we make very pretty pictures sometimes with our artfully arranged lights and shadows."

In the studio, indeed, the windows are "closed with shutters, or deeply curtained," except one, which is "partly open to a sunless portion of the sky, admitting only from high upward that partial light which, with its strongly marked contrast of shadow, is the first requisite towards seeing objects pictorially." Donatello, however, loves " 'no dark or dusky corners, except it be in a grotto, or among the thick green leaves of an arbor, or in some nook of the woods, such as I know many in the neighborhood of my home. Even there, if a stray sunbeam steal in, the shadow is all the better for its cheerful glimmer.' "

Miriam (like Zenobia not really an endearing conversationalist), inquiring, " 'And what should a boy like you—a Faun, too—know about the joys and sorrows, the intertwining light and shadow, of human life?' " offers Donatello a sketch representing a rustic dance, at which

forthwith he began to dance, and flit about the studio, like an incarnate sprite of jollity. . . . The effect in that shadowy chamber, whence the artist had so carefully excluded the sunshine, was as enlivening as if one bright ray had contrived to shimmer in the frolic around the walls, and finally rest just in the centre of the floor.

Miriam herself is a composition of intertwining light and shadow. She shows Donatello a portrait of a beautiful woman:

She was very youthful, and had what was usually thought to be a Jewish aspect; a complexion in which there was no roseate bloom, yet neither was it pale; dark eyes, into which you might look as deeply as your glance would go, and still be conscious of a depth that you had not sounded, though it lay open to the day. She had black, abundant hair, with none of the vulgar glossiness of other women's sable locks; if she were really of Jewish blood, then this was Jewish hair, and a dark glory such as crowns no Christian maiden's head.

The description is actually an accurate self-portrait of Miriam, which enraptures Donatello, though he wishes that " 'it would only smile so like the sunshine as you sometimes do.' " Seeing Miriam's smile, he adjures her to " 'let it shine upon the picture!' " She answers:

"I really half believe you are a Faun, there is such a mystery and terror for you in these dark moods, which are just as natural as daylight to us people of ordinary mould. I advise you, at all events, to look at other faces with those innocent and happy eyes, and never more to gaze at mine!"

But Donatello has taken his resolution: " 'You speak in vain; . . . shroud yourself in what gloom you will, I must needs follow you.' "

Hilda, whom Miriam now visits, is a simpler and lighter creature than Miriam (Chapter VI, "The Virgin's Shrine"). Humbler than Miriam, Hilda devotes her life to copying the works of the old Italian masters. In her métier, however, she is a genius. By her womanly "strength of heart, and by this guiding light of sympathy," she goes "straight to the central point, in which the master had conceived his work." Giving over her own prospects, she attempts only "to catch and reflect some of the glory which had been shed upon canvas from the immortal pencils of old." Her accuracy has "that evanescent and ethereal life—that flitting fragrance, as it were, of the originals—which it is as difficult to catch and retain as it would be for a sculptor to get the very movement and varying color of a living man into his marble bust."

Hilda habitually selects not the whole of a picture but some part of it

in which the spirit and essence of the picture culminated: the Virgin's celestial sorrow, for example, or a hovering angel, imbued with immortal light, or a saint with the glow of heaven in his dying face,—and these would be rendered with her whole soul. If a picture had darkened into an indistinct shadow through time and neglect, or had been injured by cleaning, or retouched by some profane hand, she seemed to possess the faculty of seeing it in its pristine glory. The copy would come from her hands with what the beholder felt must be the light which the old master had left upon the original in bestowing his final and most ethereal touch.

Hilda wins out the "glory of a great picture" by rescuing it "from the dark, chill corner of a gallery" or "from some curtained chapel in a church, where the light came seldom and aslant." From such hiding places as these she brings the "wondrous picture into daylight" and gives "all its magic splendor for the enjoyment of the world." Her self-renunciation has been wise. "Would it have been worth Hilda's while to relinquish this office for the sake of giving the world a picture or two which it would call original; pretty fancies of snow and moonlight; the counterpart in picture of so many feminine achievements in literature!" In herself she is sufficient:

> . . . pretty at all times . . . every few moments, this pretty and girlish face grew beautiful and striking, as some inward thought and feeling brightened, rose to the surface, and then, as it were, passed out of sight again; so that . . . it really seemed as if Hilda were only visible by the sunshine of her soul.

The Borghese gardens (Chapter VIII), where Donatello goes to meet Miriam, are a fusion of light and shadow, a reconciliation of art and nature, a paradise viewed from the retrospect of the Fall. As with *The Marble Faun* in general, however, the gardens' strongest effect is from art:

> The scenery amid which the youth now strayed was such as arrays itself in the imagination when we read the beautiful old myths, and fancy a brighter sky, a softer turf, a more picturesque arrangement of venerable trees, than we find in the rude and untrained landscapes of the Western world.

Amid the ilex trees, there was "never a sweeter sunshine than that now gladdening the gentle gloom which these leafy patriarchs" strive "to diffuse over the swelling and subsiding lawns." There are also, however, "avenues of cypress, resembling dark flames of huge funeral candles, which spread dusk and twilight round about them instead of cheerful radiance."

The final charm of these gardens is, strangely, the danger of malaria, which invests them with the enchantment of an aesthetic distance:

> For if you come hither in summer, and stray through these glades in the golden sunset, fever walks arm in arm with

you, and death awaits you at the end of the dim vista. Thus the scene is like Eden in its loveliness; like Eden, too, in the fatal spell that removes it beyond the scope of man's actual possessions.

The simple Donatello, however, feels "nothing of this dream-like melancholy that haunts the spot." As he passes among the "sunny shadows," his spirit seems to acquire "new elasticity." He runs races with himself "along the gleam and shadow of the wood-paths." Climbing the tallest tree, he sees beneath him "the fountains flashing in the sunlight." When he drops down and alights at Miriam's side, it is as if the "swaying of the branches" has let "a ray of sunlight through." The same ray glimmers among the "gloomy meditations" that encompass Miriam and lights up the "pale, dark beauty of her face," while it responds "pleasantly to Donatello's glance."

In Donatello's pleasure, his own mood seems to "brighten Miriam's" and is "reflected back upon himself" (Chapter IX, "The Faun and the Nymph"). He anticipates her and leads her on, running a little way ahead of her and then stopping to watch her as she approaches along the "shadowy and sun-fleckered path." She becomes vivacious, and Donatello smiles and laughs heartily, indeed, "in sympathy with the mirth" that gleams out of Miriam's "deep, dark eyes." He does not, however, "seem quite to understand her mirthful talk, nor to be disposed to explain what kind of creature" he is, knowing only "that the present moment" is "very sweet, and himself most happy, with the sunshine, the sylvan scenery, and woman's kindly charm."

Won over by his gaiety, and his avowal of love, Miriam

resolves " 'for this one hour' " to be " 'such as he imagines me. To-morrow will be time enough to come back to my reality.' " Accordingly she brightens, "as if an inward flame, heretofore stifled," is now permitted to "fill her with its happy lustre, glowing through her cheeks and dancing in her eye-beams." The two play together "like children, or creatures of immortal youth." They seem "born to be sportive forever, and endowed with eternal mirthfulness instead of any deeper joy." It is "a glimpse for backward into Arcadian life, or, further still, into the Golden Age, before mankind was burdened with sin and sorrow, and before pleasure had been darkened with those shadows that bring it into high relief, and make it happiness."

Hearing music in the distance, Miriam and Donatello begin to dance together, Miriam with "an artful beauty," her companion with "a charm of indescribable grotesqueness hand in hand with grace." At some moments, indeed, Miriam plays

> the sylvan character as perfectly as he. Catching glimpses of her, then, you would have fancied that an oak had sundered its rough bark to let her dance freely forth, endowed with the same spirit in her human form as that which rustles in the leaves; or that she had emerged through the pebbly bottom of a fountain, a water-nymph, to play and sparkle in the sunshine, flinging a quivering light around her, and suddenly disappearing in a shower of rainbow drops.

This is exquisite, but evanescent; one thinks of Pearl in the forest.

Moving toward the music, they soon draw others to join them, and fall into such merriment that it seems the Golden Age has come back again "within the precincts of this sunny glade."

> As they followed one another in a wild ring of mirth, it seemed the realization of one of those bas-reliefs where a dance of nymphs, satyrs, or bacchanals is twined around the circle of an antique vase; or it was like the sculptured scene on the front and sides of a sarcophagus, where . . . a festive procession mocks the ashes and white bones that are treasured up within.

This last reflection, however, preludes doom and sorrow. Suddenly Miriam is confronted "by a strange figure" that shakes its "fantastic garments" in the air and prances before her "on its tiptoes, almost vying with the agility of Donatello himself." It is the model. Darkness, for a moment banished, reasserts its claims. The model " 'stands in the shadow yonder,' " beckoning Miriam to follow him, and she tells Donatello that " 'your hour is past; his hour has come.' "

Left alone with her persecutor (Chapter XI, "Fragmentary Sentences"), Miriam pleads for, if not freedom, at least some brief respite. She warns him that her foreboding of their joint future is "a very dark one"—no less, in fact, than death. Thinking of their chance meeting in the catacomb of St. Calixtus, she cries, " 'Oh, that we could have wandered in those dismal passages till we both perished, taking opposite paths in the darkness, so that when we lay down to die our last breaths might not mingle!' " But the model is, like Roger Chillingworth, a gloomy fatalist; as with Chillingworth, all is to him a dark necessity. " 'In all that labyrinth of midnight paths, we should have found one another out to live or die together.' " Miriam adjures him to pray for rescue: " 'Dark as your life has been, I have known you to pray in times past!' " She warns him afresh that the end of the affair will be death, indignantly denying his hint that her words are a threat.

> "Yet," rejoined he, with a glance of dark meaning, "men have said that this white hand had once a crimson stain." He took her hand as he spoke, and held it in his own, in spite of the repugnance, amounting to nothing short of agony, with which she struggled to regain it. Holding it up to the fading light (for there was already dimness among the trees), he appeared to examine it closely, as if to discover the imaginary blood-stain with which he taunted her.

Finally, they go together toward the town, and on their way, continue to "make reference, no doubt, to some strange and dreadful history of their former life, belonging equally to this dark man and to the fair and youthful woman" whom he is persecuting.

Chapter XII, "A Stroll on the Pincian," is primarily atmospheric, although, since the Pincian Hill looks into the Borghese gardens, Hilda and Kenyon, the "strollers," see and speculate upon Donatello, Miriam, and the model as they leave the earlier scene. The sunlight is equivocal, like Rome itself, lovely, dreamlike, bathed in the past—and treacherous:

> Here sits (drooping upon some marble bench, in the treacherous sunshine) the consumptive girl, whose friends have brought her, for cure, to a climate that instils poison into its

very purest breath. . . . Here are beautiful sunsets; and here, whichever way you turn your eyes, are scenes as well worth gazing at . . . as any that the sun ever rose and set upon.

The prospect from the hill is wide, and it has the dimensions of historical and imaginative time to deepen its light. In the "blue distance" rises "Soracte, and other heights, which have gleamed afar, to our imaginations, but look scarcely real to our bodily eyes, because, being dreamed about so much, they have taken the aerial tints which belong only to a dream."

Amid this light the two onlookers talk of the three who are at the moment nearby in the Borghese. Concerning Miriam, Kenyon says: " 'Young as she is, the morning light seems already to have faded out of her life; and now comes Donatello, with natural sunshine enough for himself and her, and offers her the opportunity of making her heart and life all new and cheery again.' " Yet Kenyon, who speaks, can see in the distance the "dark follower," the "dark adversary" to whom Miriam has actually though covertly knelt in supplication. Hilda, gazing at this same tableau, fails to comprehend it. Like Donatello in the gardens, she is not able to envision darkness. Complex Rome lies before her eyes, with "its sunless alleys, and streets of palaces." It has "a gloom and languor that depress it beyond any depth of melancholic sentiment that can be elsewhere known"; yet "at this moment, the evening sunshine is flinging its golden mantle over it, making all that we thought mean magnificent." As Melville says in "The Encantadas," "The tortoise is both dark and bright," but Hilda has eyes for brightness only. As in previous scenes of *The Marble Faun*, however, the dark principle is the ending. Kenyon, seeking to overtake the model, believes that he sees him a long way ahead, but the "dusky figure" has vanished.

We turn now to moonlight (Chapter XIII, "A Sculptor's Studio"). To Hawthorne sculpture is a moonlit art of black and white, while painting engages color and the full radiance of the sun. Thematically, a relaxed account of Kenyon's studio leads eventually to the "Moonlight Ramble" (Chapter XVI) that culminates in the murder of the model. The sculptor has taxed Hilda with "the moonlit seclusion of a young girl's fancy" (Chapter XII), but his own trade is tinged with the same influence. The "pure, fine glow of the new marble" sometimes causes statuary to receive more praise than it intrinsically deserves. In this atmosphere Hilda herself takes on the touch of cold. She " 'does not dwell in our mortal atmosphere; and gentle and soft as she appears, it will be as difficult to win her heart as to entice down a white bird from its sunny freedom in the sky.' " Kenyon, however, reaches out from the limitations of his medium. His clay Cleopatra is a complex creature of sun and fire, fit to "kindle a tropic fire in the cold eyes of Octavius," a "smouldering furnace" in her heart, possessing "a certain softness and tenderness," and yet "implacable as a stone and cruel as fire." Soon, "apotheosized in an indestructible material," she will be "one of the images that men keep forever, finding a heat in them which does not cool down, throughout the centuries."

The figure clearly suggests Miriam herself, to whom

Kenyon exhibits it, and who exclaims in admiration, " 'Were you not afraid to touch her, as she grew more and more towards hot life beneath your hand? My dear friend, it is a great work!' " Indeed, Miriam is emboldened by the imaginative sympathy the work embodies to confide to Kenyon the dangerous secret that burdens her. But Coverdale-like—and perhaps wisely—he hesitates to hear it. "Unless he could give her all the sympathy, and just the kind of sympathy that the occasion required, Miriam would hate him by and by, and herself still more, if he let her speak." Complexity has its penalties, too; he has "a suspicion" that has crept into his heart and lies there "in a dark corner." Discerning this suspicion, and rebuffed, "half choked with the gush of passion" that is thus "turned back upon her," Miriam exclaims, " 'You are as cold and pitiless as your own marble.' " Art, it would seem, is not life; and perhaps Kenyon has not wholly escaped the limitations of his medium after all.

In a further discussion of art, the author regrets that he must "forgo the delight of illuminating this chapter with personal allusions to men whose renown glows richly on canvas, or gleams in the white moonlight of marble" (Chapter XV, "An Aesthetic Company"). The "pure, white, undecaying substance" of marble imposes a particular responsibility: "It insures immortality to whatever is wrought in it, and therefore makes it a religious obligation to commit no idea to its mighty guardianship, save such as may repay the marble for its faithful care, its incorruptible fidelity, by warming it with an ethereal life." Yet some rough sketches are more impressive than creations embodied in marble. "There is an effluence of divinity in the first sketch; and there, if anywhere, you find the pure light of inspiration, which the subsequent toil of the artist serves to bring out in stronger lustre, indeed, but likewise adulterates it with what belongs to an inferior mood."

As earlier in the Borghese gardens and on the Pincian Hill, here light gives way to darkness at the last, since among these rough drawings is what Hilda takes to be "the original sketch for the picture of the Archangel Michael setting his foot upon the demon, in the Church of Cappuccini." The demon of the sketch is entirely unlike and, as Kenyon says, " 'a more energetic demon, altogether, than that of the finished picture.' " It is, as the viewers gradually realize, a good likeness of Miriam's model. Is it, "an actual portrait of somebody, that haunted the old master," as Miriam is haunted now? "Did the ominous shadow follow him through all the sunshine of his earlier career, and into the gloom that gathered about its close?" The four friends, Hilda, Kenyon, Donatello, and Miriam, agree to visit the Church of the Cappuccini the next morning to examine the finished picture—which, we find later on, is striking very close to home for the model. Meanwhile, the four propose a "ramble through the streets, taking in their way some of those scenes of ruin" which produce their 'best effects under the splendor of the Italian moon."

Roman moonlight, like Roman sunlight, is special. It has a little more color and depth and more potentialities of distancing, symmetry, and contrast than ordinary moonlight. Going outdoors, the four look upward and see the sky "full of light" which seems to have a "delicate purple or crimson lustre, or, at least, some richer tinge than the cold, white moonshine of other skies." Moonlight emphasizes, picking out outlines and contrasts, in figure showing forth the splendor and the misery of Rome. It gleams over the "front of the opposite palace, showing the architectural ornaments of its cornice and pillared portal, as well as the iron-barred basement-windows" that give "such a prison-like aspect to the structure, and the shabbiness and squalor" that lie along its base. The Fountain of Trevi is an "untamable water, sporting by itself in the moonshine, and compelling all the elaborate trivialities of art to assume a natural aspect, in accordance with its own powerful simplicity."

Miriam, remembering an incident from Mme de Staël's *Corinne*, wants to see if a reflected face can be recognized in the water. It proves impossible: the moon flings "Miriam's shadow to the bottom of the fountain, as well as two more shadows of persons" who have followed her, "on either side."

> "Three shadows!" exclaimed Miriam. "Three separate shadows, all so black and heavy that they sink in the water! There they lie on the bottom, as if all three were drowned together. This shadow on my right is Donatello; I know him by his curls, and the turn of his head. My left-hand companion puzzles me; a shapeless mass, as indistinct as the premonition of calamity! Which of you can it be? Ah!"

It is, of course, the ubiquitous model. Half-jokingly—because of her companions—Miriam tries to exorcise him with water from the fountain. " 'In the name of all the Saints,' " she cries, " 'vanish, Demon, and let me be free of you now and forever!' " Her attempt, however, is "quite ineffectual upon the pertinacious demon, or whatever the apparition might be."

The excursion continues, amid famous places. At length the company arrives at the Coliseum (Chapter XVII, "Miriam's Trouble") within which the moonlight fills and floods the "great empty space"; it glows upon "tier above tier of ruined, grass-grown arches" and makes them "even too distinctly visible."

> The splendor of the revelation took away that inestimable effect of dimness and mystery by which the imagination might be assisted to build a grander structure than the Coliseum, and to shatter it with a more picturesque decay. Byron's celebrated description is better than the reality. He beheld the scene in his mind's eye, through the witchery of many intervening years, and faintly illuminated it as if with starlight instead of this broad glow of moonshine.

Prominent in the light, however, is the great black cross, "where, thousands of times over, the dying gladiator fell."

The company of artists sit "enjoying the moonlight and shadow, the present gayety and the gloomy reminiscences of the scene, in almost equal share." It is remarked that artists "are lifted by the ideality of their pursuits a little way off the earth. . . ." They are able to "partake somewhat more bountifully than other people in the thin delights of moonshine and romance." Again, however, the model interposes; he is recognized by "the moonshine on his face" as he goes round the circle of shrines. At sight of him Miriam shrinks back "into the deep obscurity of an

arch." Thinking herself alone, she gives way, but Donatello has followed her, and witnesses a spectacle that has
"its own kind of horror":

> ... the beautiful Miriam began to gesticulate extravagantly,
> gnashing her teeth, flinging her arms wildly abroad, stamp-
> ing with her foot. It was as if she had stepped aside for an
> instant, solely to snatch the relief of a brief fit of madness.

When the horrified Donatello makes his presence known,
she solemnly bids him, " 'Cast me off, or you are lost forever.' " He is, however, unshakably loyal: a "higher sentiment" brightens "upon Donatello's face" than has "hitherto
seemed to belong to its simple expression and sensuous
beauty." The girl accepts his aid, though reflecting what
a sin it is " 'to stain his joyous nature with the blackness of
a woe like mine!' "

The company goes on to the Forum (Chapter XVIII,
"On the Edge of a Precipice") stopping at the place Kenyon describes as " 'the spot where the chasm opened, into
which Curtius precipitated his good steed and himself.
Imagine the great, dusky gap, impenetrably deep, and with
half-shaped monsters and hideous faces looming upward
out of it.' " Moralizing upon it, Miriam remarks, " 'The
chasm was merely one of the orifices of that pit of blackness
that lies beneath us, everywhere.' " Another chasm divides
the Forum from the modern mind, the author adds, extend-
ing "between it and ourselves, in which lie all those dark,
rude, unlettered centuries, around the birth-time of Chris-
tianity, as well as the age of chivalry and romance, the
feudal system, and the infancy of a better civilization than

that of Rome." Structurally, however, this talk of dark chasms is leading to the gulf into which the model is shortly to fall, into a blackness that will cover his slayers as well.

Meanwhile we are led climactically to the chief glory of ancient Rome, the equestrian statue of Marcus Aurelius. Significantly, considering the passage just quoted, on "the infancy of a better civilization," the great pagan is beheld by moonlight, which glistens upon "traces of the gilding which once covered both rider and steed." These traces are almost gone, but the "aspect of dignity" is "still perfect, clothing the figure as it were with an imperial robe of light." Aurelius is "the most majestic representation of the kingly character that ever the world has seen." His is a "command" that is in itself a "benediction." A yet greater reverence, however, is reserved for the statue of Pope Julius at Perugia, which Miriam, Donatello, and Kenyon are later to view in the sun.

Finally the company comes to the ill-omened "Traitor's Leap" from the Tarpeian Rock, where Kenyon bids his friends, " 'Look over the parapet, and see what a sheer tumble there might still be for a traitor, in spite of the thirty feet of soil that have accumulated at the foot of the precipice.' " From an angle of the parapet there is a "precipitous plunge straight downward into a stone-paved court." The four suddenly realize that it is midnight and that they are literally, as one of them says, " 'dreaming on the edge of a precipice.' " They decide that it is time to go home.

It is in this setting that the model is killed. Miriam finds everyone gone, except for herself and Donatello "hanging over the brow of the ominous precipice." But "in the basement wall of the palace, shaded from the moon," there is a "deep, empty niche" from which a figure emerges and comes toward Miriam. There is a sudden, brief, dreamlike struggle, and the model is dashed upon the stone below. Donatello has committed the act, and Miriam has furnished the motivation—by one glance of which she herself is unconscious. And the innocent Hilda, who has come back to look for her two friends, is the unseen witness of the act.

The succeeding chapters—perhaps the remainder of the novel—constitute an elaborate investigation of the psychology of guilt. Donatello, the genial product of sunshine, is now all fire (Chapter XIX, "The Faun's Transformation"). His eyes blaze with the "fierce energy" that has "suddenly inspired him." It has "kindled him into a man"; it has "developed within him an intelligence which was no native characteristic of the Donatello whom we have heretofore known." But that "simple and joyous creature" is "gone forever." The "glow of rage" is "still lurid on Donatello's face" and flashes "out again from his eyes." As for the bemused Miriam:

> . . . she could not deny—she was not sure whether it might be so, or no—that a wild joy had flamed up in her heart, when she beheld her persecutor in his mortal peril. . . . Be the emotion what it might, it had blazed up more madly, when Donatello flung his victim off the cliff, and more and more, while his shriek went quivering downward.

Meanwhile, the victim is a "dark mass, lying in a heap" below them, an image that recalls his shadow in the Fountain of Trevi.

The first reaction of the guilty pair is a sense of freedom and exaltation:

They flung the past behind them... or else distilled from it a fiery intoxication, which sufficed to carry them triumphantly through those first moments of their doom. For, guilt has its moment of rapture too. The foremost result of a broken law is ever an ecstatic sense of freedom. And thus there exhaled upward (out of their dark sympathy, at the base of which lay a human corpse) a bliss, or an insanity, which the unhappy pair imagined to be well worth the sleepy innocence that was forever lost to them.

Miriam is conscious that the feeling is transitory, but says, " 'To-night, at least, there shall be no remorse!' " Wandering at random, they come to Hilda's tower. There is a "light in her high chamber; a light, too, at the Virgin's shrine; and the glimmer of these two" is "the loftiest light beneath the stars." Seeing Hilda at the window, Miriam calls out to her, but the window is immediately closed, and Hilda disappears "from behind the snowy curtain."

In what ensues, the fire that has taken the place of sunshine in Donatello dies away. "How icy cold is the heart, when the fervor, the wild ecstasy of passion, has faded away, and sunk down among the dead ashes of the fire that blazed so fiercely, and was fed by the very substance of its life!" (Chapter XX, "The Burial Chant"). Observing Donatello, Kenyon notes how entirely the "fine, fresh glow of animal spirits" has departed from his face. "All his youthful gayety, and with it his simplicity of manner," is "eclipsed, if not utterly extinct." Miriam leads Donatello "to the gardens of the Villa Medici, hoping that the quiet shade and sunshine of that delightful retreat" will "a little revive his spirits" (Chapter XXII, "The Medici Gardens"). But Donatello draws "no delight from these things." The sun itself betrays him, for "a brown lizard with two tails—a monster often engendered by the Roman sunshine—" runs across his foot and makes him start.

The two part, and Miriam turns to Hilda for solace (Chapter XXIII, "Miriam and Hilda"). But Hilda's life has also been darkened by the crime. She watches a "speck of sunshine" that comes through a shuttered window and creeps "from object to object, indicating each with a touch of its bright finger, and then letting them all vanish successively. In like manner, her mind, so like sunlight in its natural cheerfulness," goes "from thought to thought" but finds nothing that it can "dwell upon for comfort." In her despair Miriam tries to disguise herself in light: she visits Hilda "in a garb of sunshine," and is disclosed, as the door opens, "in all the glow of her remarkable beauty." She is rebuffed; Hilda pleads that she is too simple and too weak to help. " 'Your powerful magnetism would be too much for me. The pure, white atmosphere, in which I try to discern what things are good and true, would be discolored. . . . Your deed, Miriam, has darkened the whole sky!' "

From the obsessive atmosphere of the murder the book moves to clearer air and wider landscapes, filtered through the artist's vision of Kenyon, a relatively disengaged observer. In summer the artist leaves Rome and goes to "pour, if he can, the purple air of Italy over his canvas" and "to walk the long, bright galleries of Florence, or to steal glowing colors from the miraculous works, which he finds in a score of Venetian palaces" (Chapter XXIV, "The Tower Among the Apennines"). "This sunny, shadowy, breezy, wandering life, in which he seeks for beauty as his treasure, and gathers for his winter's honey what is but a passing fragrance to all other men, is worth living for, come afterwards what may." After a leisurely tour Kenyon comes at length to Donatello's castle in the Apennines, the Tower of Monte Beni. While seeking entrance to the closed tower, the sun is so hot that "the unsheltered traveller" shouts "another impatient summons." As he remarks to the finally aroused Donatello: " 'This is a warm reception, truly! Pray bid your porter let me in, before the sun shrivels me quite into a cinder.' " Donatello has "a stern and sorrowful look in his eyes" which has "altered his youthful face as if it had seen thirty years of trouble." Inside the tower he apologizes to his guest for the darkness of the surroundings: " 'I see you already find the old house dismal' " (Chapter XXV, "Sunshine"). Donatello offers an antidote, a wine called Sunshine, " 'the secret of making which has been kept in our family for centuries upon centuries.' " He invites the sculptor to taste it, adding: " 'But first smell its fragrance; for the wine is very lavish of it, and will scatter it all abroad.' "

The wine, pale golden in hue, is peculiarly subtle and evanescent, demanding "so deliberate a pause, in order to detect the hidden peculiarities and subtile exquisiteness of its flavor," that the drink it is "really more a moral than a physical enjoyment." There is a "deliciousness" in it that eludes analysis. Its qualities are highly transitory, so that if one lingers too long in drinking it it becomes "disenchanted both of its fragrance and its flavor." It rather resembles, indeed, the happiness that Clifford Pyncheon seeks so wistfully—or, closer to home, the "thin delights" and the "passing fragrance" of the beauty that is the artist's treasure. The wine is notable for its luster: as it stands in Kenyon's glass, a "little circle of light" glows "on the table round about it," as if it is "really so much golden sunshine."

Kenyon suggests to Donatello that " 'the pale, liquid gold, in every such flask as that, might be solidified into golden scudi, and would quickly make you a millionaire!' " However, the butler replies that according to tradition " 'this rare wine of our vineyard would lose all its wonderful qualities, if any of it were sent to market. The Counts of Monte Beni have never parted with a single flask of it for gold.' " He adds, more matter-of-factly, that the wine " 'is so fond of its native home, that a transportation of even a few miles turns it quite sour.' " Yet it " 'keeps well in the cellar, underneath this floor, and gathers fragrance, flavor, and brightness, in its dark dungeon.' " Plainly Sunshine has some likeness to Donatello himself, who has suffered from exposure to a wider and bleaker reality than his native and ancestral tower. As for the "dark dungeon," the image may give some hope for his ultimate disposition.

The room in which Donatello entertains his guest is splendid, but dimmed by age. In earlier days it "must have presented an aspect both gorgeous and enlivening," for it invests "some of the cheerfullest ideas and emotions of which the human mind is susceptible with the external reality of beautiful form, and rich, harmonious glow and variety of color." The ancient frescos, however, are perhaps the more melancholy for their original cheerfulness:

". . . the closer their resemblance to the happy past, the gloomier now." Kenyon, whose spirits are "still upheld by the mild potency of the Monte Beni wine," declares:

> "Your forefathers, my dear Count, must have been joyous fellows, keeping up the vintage merriment throughout the year. It does me good to think of them gladdening the hearts of men and women, with their wine of Sunshine, even in the Iron Age, as Pan and Bacchus, whom we see yonder, did in the Golden one!"

But Donatello's vision has darkened: " '. . . when I brought my own cheerfulness into the saloon, these frescos looked cheerful too. But, methinks, they have all faded since I saw them last.' "

The family of Monte Beni has lived upon the site "for immemorial ages. And there they . . . laid the foundations of their tower, so long ago that one half of its height was said to be sunken under the surface and to hide subterranean chambers which once were cheerful with the olden sunshine." According to legend, they were of "the same happy and poetic kindred who dwelt in Arcadia, and—whether they ever lived such life or not—enriched the world with dreams, at least, and fables, lovely, if unsubstantial, of a Golden Age." They were "strong, active, genial, cheerful as the sunshine, passionate as the tornado. Their lives were rendered blissful by an unsought harmony with nature" (Chapter XXVI, "The Pedigree of Monte Beni").

In time the family qualities were vitiated; but according to his tenants, Donatello is a true scion of his ancient race: "Their hovels had always glowed like sunshine when he entered them; so that, as the peasants expressed it, their young master had never darkened a doorway in his life. He was the soul of vintage festivals." He has changed, however, and Kenyon inquires of the butler Tomaso whether he, too, has noticed the "shadow" which is "said to have fallen over Donatello's life." The servant replies:

> "The world has grown either too evil, or else too wise and sad, for such men as the old Counts of Monte Beni used to be. His very first taste of it, as you see, has changed and spoilt my poor young lord. . . . now it brings the tears into my eyes to hear him sighing over a cup of Sunshine!"

Kenyon comfortingly suggests that " 'this will be a famous year for the golden wine of Monte Beni. As long as your grapes produce that admirable liquor, sad as you think the world, neither the Count nor his guests will quite forget to smile.' " Donatello, however, " 'scarcely wets his lips with the sunny juice.' " Kenyon himself is disposed to seek comfort in the golden wine, and, "to say the truth," it is "no unnecessary ingredient towards making the life of Monte Beni palatable." It seems "a pity" that Donatello does not "drink a little more of it, and go jollily to bed at least, even if he should awake with an accession of darker melancholy the next morning." Despite all expedients, a cloud seems to hang over "these once Arcadian precincts" and "to be darkest around the summit of the tower" where Donatello is "wont to sit and brood."

The young count tells Kenyon of an ancestor of his, beloved by a fountain nymph, "a fresh, cool, dewy thing, sunny and shadowy." It was her agreeable habit to

suddenly fall down around him in a shower of sunny raindrops, with a rainbow glancing through them, and forthwith gather herself up into the likeness of a beautiful girl. . . . Thus, kind maiden that she was, the hot atmosphere became deliciously cool and fragrant for this favored knight.

" 'It is a delightful story for the hot noon of your Tuscan summer,' " observes the sculptor at this point. " 'But the deportment of the watery lady must have had a most chilling influence in midwinter.' " However this may be, the chief point of the tale is the desertion of the young knight by his fountain lady when he seeks to wash away the stain of murder in her waters, which is immediately paralleled in reality by Donatello's own failure to call to himself the creatures of the neighboring fields and woods. Kenyon, the onlooker, sees "no living thing, save a brown lizard . . . of the tarantula species . . . rustling away through the sunshine. To all present appearance, this venomous reptile" is the only creature that responds to the young count's efforts to "renew his intercourse with the lower orders of nature." One recalls the brown lizard with two tails that disturbed him in the Medici gardens in Rome.

There is a sweeping view from the summit of the Tower of Monte Beni, which Kenyon persuades Donatello to show him. As the sententious Kenyon remarks, " '. . . with its difficult steps, and the dark prison-cells . . . your tower resembles the spiritual experience of many a sinful soul, which, nevertheless, may struggle upward into the pure air and light of Heaven at last!' " Emerging into the open, the sculptor feels as if his being is "suddenly magnified a hundred-fold." For there is "the broad, sunny smile of God, which we fancy to be spread over that favored land more abundantly than on other regions," and beneath it glows "a most rich and varied fertility." Amid "this spacious map" lakes open "their blue eyes in its face, reflecting heaven, lest mortals should forget that better land" when they behold "the earth so beautiful." A thunderstorm is approaching, but behind it brightens forth again "the sunny splendor."

To the sculptor the majestic and varied landscape is a vision of unity and beneficence:

> "Thank God for letting me again behold this scene! . . . I have viewed it from many points, and never without as full a sensation of gratitude as my heart seems capable of feeling. How it strengthens the poor human spirit in its reliance on His providence, to ascend but this little way above the common level, and so attain a somewhat wider glimpse of His dealings with mankind! He doeth all things right! His will be done!"

Donatello sees only an incomprehensible duality: " '. . . sunshine on one spot, and cloud in another, and no reason for it in either case. The sun on you; the cloud on me!' " But to Kenyon there is

> "a page of heaven and a page of earth spread wide open before us! Only begin to read it, and you will find it interpreting itself without the aid of words. . . . When we ascend into the higher regions of emotion and spiritual enjoyment, they are only expressible by such grand hieroglyphics as these around us."

Still on the summit (Chapter XXIX, "On the Battlements"), Kenyon speaks casually of the impulse to leap from high places. He has, of course, no conception of an application to Donatello, who clings to life " 'in a way which you cannot conceive; it has been so rich, so warm, so sunny!—and beyond its verge, nothing but the chilly dark! And then a fall from a precipice is such an awful death!' " Kenyon, "not without an unshaped suspicion of the definite fact," knows that Donatello's condition "must have resulted from the weight and gloom of life":

> It was perceptible that he had already had glimpses of strange and subtle matters in those dark caverns, into which all men must descend, if they would know anything beneath the surface and illusive pleasures of existence. And when they emerge, though dazzled and blinded by the first glare of daylight, they take truer and sadder views of life forever afterwards.

The thunderstorm has left the sky "heavy with tumbling vapors, interspersed with . . . tracts of blue, vividly brightened by the sun." In the east lies "a dusky region of cloud and sullen mist. . . . Far into this misty cloud-region, however,—within the domain of chaos, as it were,—hilltops" are seen "brightening in the sunshine"; they look like "fragments of the world, broken adrift and based on nothingness." The sculptor, thinking as a plastic artist, fancies that the scene represents "the process of the Creator, when he held the new, imperfect earth in his hand, and modelled it." Kenyon speaks of the magic and variety of clouds in mountain scenery, and their suggestiveness. Donatello " 'can see cloud-shapes, too,' " but, true to his dark vision, he interprets the one before him as " 'the figure of a monk reclining, with his cowl about his head and drawn partly over his face.' " It is, in fact, the dead model lying in the Church of the Cappuccini.

At sunset the scene is "tenderly magnificent, with mild gradations of hue, and a lavish outpouring of gold, but rather such gold as we see on the leaf of a bright flower than the burnished glow of metal from the mine." Or. "if metallic," it looks "airy and unsubstantial, like the glorified dreams of an alchemist." Night comes on swiftly, and Kenyon finds in its starlight a parallel with Donatello, whose face as they converse brightens "beneath the stars." He is no longer the Faun of the Capitol, but "the original beauty," which sorrow has "partly effaced," comes back "elevated and spiritualized." In "the black depths" the Faun has "found a soul" and is "struggling with it towards the light of heaven." It must be added, however, that "the illumination" soon fades from Donatello's face.

The summer advances, and vintage time arrives. The peasants find ripe grapes for Kenyon, "in every little globe of which" is included a "fragrant draught of the sunny Monte Beni wine" (Chapter XXX, "Donatello's Bust"). The process of wine making has "a flavor of poetry" about it, unlike "the labor that is devoted in sad, hard earnest to raise grain for sour bread." The "sunburnt young men and dark-cheeked, laughing girls" who weed the fields might pass for "inhabitants of an unsophisticated Arcadia." The scene is darkened, however, by the "remorseful anguish" of Donatello; and Kenyon has his own pain, in the "never-quiet, never-satisfied yearning of his heart towards Hilda." Yet it is possible that "even Donatello's grief and Kenyon's pale, sunless affection" lend a charm to Monte Beni "which it would not have retained amid a more abundant joyousness." As in the Borghese gardens, darkness outlines and mellows the light. The sculptor has somewhat the sensations of an adventurer who should find his way to the site of ancient Eden, and behold its loveliness through the transparency of that gloom which has been brooding over those haunts of innocence ever since the fall. Adam saw it in a brighter sunshine, but never knew the shade of pensive beauty which Eden won from his expulsion.

Kenyon now interviews Miriam, who has been waiting in the background for an opportunity to repair the harm she has inflicted upon the sunny Donatello (Chapter XXXI, "The Marble Saloon"). They meet in a "rich hall of Monte Beni," hitherto unseen by Kenyon, splendid in "polished and richly colored marble," of a sort that

> shines indestructibly, and, with a little dusting, looks just as brilliant in its three hundredth year as the day after the final slab of giallo antico was fitted into the wall. To the sculptor, at this first view of it, it seemed a hall where the sun was magically imprisoned, and must always shine. He anticipated Miriam's entrance, arrayed in queenly robes, and beaming with even more than the singular beauty that had heretofore distinguished her.

Instead she is "very pale, and dressed in deep mourning." Feeble and ill with despair, she takes heart at Kenyon's assurance that Donatello loves her still. Kenyon, they decide, will persuade the count to join him on a tour, and Miriam will meet them as if by accident along the way. She decides upon "the bronze statue of Pope Julius in the great square of Perugia" as a fitting rendezvous. She says:

> "I remember standing in the shadow of that statue one sunny noontime, and being impressed by its paternal aspect, and fancying that a blessing fell upon me from its out-

stretched hand. Ever since, I have had a superstition . . . that, if I waited long enough in that same spot, some good event would come to pass."

The appointment is accordingly made for a fortnight after the tour begins. Miriam says, " '. . . bring Donatello, at noon, to the base of the statue.' "

Before leaving, Kenyon climbs the tower again and watches "a sunset and a moonrise over the great valley." On the evening before his departure he drinks "one flask, and then another, of the Monte Beni Sunshine" and stores up its flavor in his memory, "as the standard of what is exquisite in wine" (Chapter XXXII, "Scenes by the Way"). Setting forth on horseback, the two travelers decide to "perform much of their aimless journeyings under the moon, and in the cool of the morning or evening twilight." The midday sun, though summer has hardly begun to "trail its departing skirts over Tuscany," is still "too fervid to allow of noontide exposure." Later they see before them

> the broad valley, with a mist so thinly scattered over it as to be perceptible only in the distance, and most so in the nooks and the hills. Now that we have called it mist, it seems a mistake not rather to have called it sunshine; the glory of so much light being mingled with so little gloom, in the airy material of that vapor. Be it mist or sunshine, it adds a touch of ideal beauty to the scene, almost persuading the spectator that this valley and those hills are visionary, because their visible atmosphere is so like the substance of a dream.

By way of contrast, "As usual, on Italian waysides," the wanderers pass "great, black crosses, hung with all the instruments of the sacred agony and passion." Thus, while the "fertile scene" shows the "never-failing beneficence of the Creator towards man in his transitory state," these symbols remind each wayfarer of "the Saviour's infinitely greater love for him as an immortal spirit." Miriam, who is surreptitiously following the travelers, is "an invisible companion," like a dream that has "strayed out of their slumber," and is "haunting them in the daytime, when its shadowy substance" can have "neither density nor outlines, in the too obtrusive light." After sunset, the shadow grows "a little more distinct."

On their leisurely way they enter many churches, and Kenyon's interest is notably engaged by the stained-glass windows (Chapter XXXIII, "Pictured Windows"):

> It is the special excellence of pictured glass, that the light, which falls merely on the outside of other pictures, is here interfused throughout the work; it illuminates the design, and invests it with a living radiance; and in requital the unfading colors transmute the common daylight into a miracle of richness and glory in its passage through the heavenly substance of the blessed and angelic shapes which throng the high-arched window.

Of these "frail yet enduring and fadeless pictures," the sculptor exclaims that " 'there is no other such true symbol of the glories of the better world, where a celestial radiance will be inherent in all things and persons, and render each continually transparent to the sight of all.' " " 'But what a horror it would be,' " says Donatello, sadly, " 'if there were a soul among them through which the light could not be transfused!' " The sculptor replies that "perhaps this is to be the punishment of sin . . . not that it shall be made evident to the universe . . . but that it shall insulate the sinner from all sweet society by rendering him impermeable to light, and, therefore, unrecognizable in the abode of heavenly simplicity and truth. Then, what remains for him, but the dreariness of infinite and eternal solitude?"

Miriam, "a figure in a dark robe . . . lurking in the obscurity of a side-chapel close by," makes an "impulsive movement" toward Donatello, but shrinks back and is "quite lost to sight among the shadows of the chapel" at his reply to Kenyon, devastating to her: " '. . . there might be a more miserable torture than to be solitary forever. . . . Think of having a single companion in eternity, and instead of finding any consolation, or at all events variety of torture, to see your own weary, weary sin repeated in that inseparable soul.' "

Kenyon, commenting on Milton's phrase, "dim, religious light," remarks of a window that " 'the pictures are most brilliant in themselves, yet dim with tenderness and reverence, because God himself is shining through them.' " Donatello, however, trembles " 'at those awful saints; and, most of all, at the figure above them. He glows with Divine wrath!' " To the sculptor's assertion that " 'it is divine love, not wrath!' " he flatly dissents, adding that " 'each must interpret for himself.' " From outside the window nothing is visible "but the merest outline of dusky shapes. . . . That miracle of radiant art, thus viewed," is "nothing better than an incomprehensible obscurity, without a gleam of beauty to induce the beholder to attempt unravelling it." " 'Christian faith,' " thinks Kenyon to himself, " 'is a grand cathedral, with divinely pictured windows. Standing without, you see no glory, nor can possibly imagine any; standing within, every ray of light reveals a harmony of unspeakable splendors.' "

These passages doubtless anticipate the reunion of Donatello and Miriam in Perugia, beneath the beneficent hand of the statue of Pope Julius. The travelers reach the town before the sun has "quite kissed away the early freshness of the morning." A heavy rain has enlivened "the scene of verdure and fertility amid which this ancient civilization stands. Kenyon loiters when they come to the "gray city-wall" and is "loath to give up the prospect of the sunny wilderness" that lies below. The situation is "as green as England, and bright as Italy alone." There is "all the wide valley, sweeping down and spreading away on all sides from the weed-grown ramparts, and bounded afar by mountains," which lies "asleep in the sun, with thin mists and silvery clouds floating about their heads by way of morning dreams." Perugia is a place of mild and harmonious contrasts—its gray stone against natural green and gold; the "gray solemnity" and the "shadow of the cathedral and other old Gothic structures" that give "shelter from the sunshine"; and the quiet, majestic patience of the great statue of Pope Julius in the midst of the cheerful stir and the shifting variousness of the market-place (Chapter XXXIV, "Market-Day in Perugia").

High noon is to be "Miriam's hour," and she faces the test equipped with "a beauty that might be imagined bright enough to glimmer with its own light in a dim cathedral aisle," and has "no need to shrink from the severer test of the mid-day sun" (Chapter XXXV, "The Bronze Pontiff's Benediction"). She has probably "planned this momentous interview, on so public a spot and at high noon, with an eye to the sort of protection that would be thrown over it by a multitude of eye-witnesses." She avows to Donatello once more her grief that, " 'encountering so rare a being, and gifted with the power of sympathy with his sunny life, it was my doom, mine, to bring him within the limits of sinful, sorrowful mortality!' " Both hesitate; two souls are "groping for each other in the darkness of guilt and sorrow," and are hardly "bold enough to grasp the cold hands" that they find. They draw together, however, and see the "majestic figure" of Pope Julius "stretching out the hand of benediction over them, and bending down upon this guilty and repentant pair its vision of grand benignity."

Meanwhile Hilda, alone in Rome, is shrouded in the atmosphere of the crime she has witnessed (Chapter XXXVI, "Hilda's Tower"). She is suffering from the "dismal certainty of the existence of evil in the world," a "sad mystery. . . . When that knowledge comes, it is as if a cloud had suddenly gathered over the morning light; so dark a cloud, that there seems to be no longer any sunshine behind or above it." She is enveloped in an "awful loneliness." It is "a shadow in the sunshine of festal days; a mist between her eyes and the pictures" at which she strives to look, "a chill dungeon," which keeps her in its "gray twilight" and feeds her with its "unwholesome air." In vain she seeks help in the picture galleries (Chapter XXXVII, "The Emptiness of Picture Galleries"):

There was no more of that cheery alacrity with which she used to flit upward, as if her doves had lent her their wings, nor of that glow of happy spirits which had been wont to set the tarnished gilding of the picture-frames and the shabby splendor of the furniture all a-glimmer, as she hastened to her congenial and delightful toil.

She becomes for the first time acquainted "with that icy demon of weariness, who haunts great picture galleries, . . . a plausible Mephistopheles" who "annihilates color, warmth, and more especially, sentiment and passion, at a touch." The author remarks:

A picture, however admirable the painter's art, and wonderful his power, requires of the spectator a surrender of himself, in due proportion with the miracle which has been wrought. Let the canvas glow as it may, you must look with the eye of faith, or its highest excellence escapes you. There is always the necessity of helping out the painter's art with your own resources of sensibility and imagination.

These resources Hilda has lost.

Hilda turns next to "Altars and Incense" (Chapter XXXVIII). The Roman Catholic faith

marvellously adapts itself to every human need. . . . It supplies a multitude of external forms, in which the spiritual may be clothed and manifested; it has many painted windows, as it were, through which the celestial sunshine, else disregarded, may make itself gloriously perceptible in visions of beauty and splendor.

Hilda enters upon a pilgrimage among the Roman altars and shrines:

She climbed the hundred steps of the Ara Coeli; she trod the broad, silent nave of St. John Lateran; she stood in the Pantheon, under the round opening in the dome, through which the blue sunny sky still gazes down, as it used to gaze when there were Roman deities in the antique niches.

Seeking a fitting deity, she looks especially among representations of the Virgin, but never finds quite what she wants, "a face of celestial beauty, but human as well as heavenly, and with the shadow of past grief upon it; bright with immortal youth, yet matronly and motherly."

At last and inevitably she comes to St. Peter's, which she has hitherto misprized as wanting in sublimity. She has imagined

> a structure of no definite outline ... dim and gray and huge, stretching into an interminable perspective, and over-arched by a dome like the cloudy firmament. . . . So, in her earlier visits, when the compassed splendor of the actual interior glowed before her eyes, she had profanely called it a great prettiness.

Now, in her trouble, she sees it with new eyes. One afternoon, as Hilda enters St. Peter's "in sombre mood," its interior beams upon her "with all the effect of a new creation." It seems "an embodiment of whatever the imagination could conceive, or the heart desire, as a magnificent, comprehensive, majestic symbol of the religious faith." All splendor is included "within its verge," and there is "space for all." There is "manifold magnificence" here, "enough to have made world-famous shrines in any other church," but which here melts away into the "vast sunny breadth," to become "of no separate account."

Heavenly light streams from the dome. "Rich, gorgeous, filled with sunshine, cheerfully sublime, and fadeless after centuries," those "lofty depths" seem to "translate the heavens to mortal comprehension, and help the spirit upward to a yet higher and wider sphere." Hilda, "the daughter of Puritan forefathers," is repelled by the "gaudy superstitions" about her. "Seeing a woman, a priest, and a soldier kneel to kiss the toe of the brazen St. Peter, who protrudes it beyond his pedestal, for the purpose, polished bright with former salutations," while a child stands on tiptoe "to do the same," the glory of the church is "darkened before Hilda's eyes." Nevertheless, led onward by "a mosaic copy of Guido's beautiful Archangel, treading on the prostrate fiend," she suddenly finds herself kneeling in prayer before the shrine of St. Michael. There is "a strange sense of relief won by that momentary, passionate prayer," and "a hope, born of hysteric trouble," flutters in her heart. It is not, however, hopefully described. "The unhappy are continually tantalized by similar delusions of succor near at hand; at least, the despair is very dark that has no such will-o'-the-wisp to glimmer in it."

Yet there is much light in the church of a genuine nature (Chapter XXXIX, "The World's Cathedral"):

> Still gliding onward, Hilda now looked up into the dome, where the sunshine came through the western windows, and threw across long shafts of light. They rested upon the mosaic figures of two evangelists above the cornice. These great beams of radiance, traversing what seemed the empty space, were made visible in misty glory, by the holy cloud of incense, else unseen, which had risen into the middle dome. It was to Hilda as if she beheld the worship of the priest and people ascending heavenward, purified from its alloy of earth, and acquiring celestial substance in the golden atmos-

phere to which it aspired. She wondered if angels did not sometimes hover within the dome, and show themselves, in brief glimpses, floating amid the sunshine and the glorified vapor, to those who devoutly worshipped on the pavement.

The girl at length reveals her secret in confession, a sacrament to which she has no right and which in any event is unacceptable to her as such. Nevertheless, at the end she kneels to receive the blessing "with as devout a simplicity as any Catholic of them all."

This act is witnessed with great uneasiness by Kenyon, who has returned to Rome and has been looking for her (Chapter XL, "Hilda and a Friend"). He misinterprets her action; and Hilda's demeanor, in her "peaceful beatitude," prolongs his misconception: "While coming towards him in the solemn radiance which, at that period of the day, is diffused through the transept, and showered down beneath the dome," she seems "of the same substance" as the atmosphere that envelops her. He can hardly tell whether she is "imbued with sunshine" or whether it is a "glow of happiness" that shines out of her. So changed is she that it is as if

one of the throng of angelic people, who might be hovering in the sunny depths of the dome, had alighted on the pavement. Indeed, this capability of transfiguration, which we often see wrought by inward delight on persons far less capable of it than Hilda, suggests how angels come by their beauty. It grows out of their happiness, and lasts forever only because that is immortal.

In her relief Hilda's heart seems so full that it spills "its new gush of happiness, as it were, like rich and sunny wine out of an over-brimming goblet." Kenyon, still supposing her converted or near conversion to Roman Catholicism, sets himself to argue against it. St. Peter's, he says, should have painted windows, not clear glass:

> "Daylight, in its natural state, ought not to be admitted here. It should stream through a brilliant illusion of saints and hierarchies, and old scriptural images, and symbolized dogmas, purple, blue, golden, and a broad flame of scarlet. Then, it would be just such an illumination as the Catholic faith allows to its believers. But, give me—to live and die in—the pure, white light of heaven!"

Hilda, avowing, " 'I love the white light too!' " nevertheless expresses sympathy with Catholic worship, though no commitment to it. "Before leaving the church, Hilda and Kenyon turn "to admire again its mighty breadth, the remoteness of the glory behind the altar, and the effect of visionary splendor and magnificence imparted by the long bars of smoky sunshine," which travel "so far before arriving at a place of rest." Hilda, perhaps affected by this last, exclaims, " 'Thank Heaven for having brought me hither!' " A little later she makes a remark about the seven-branched candlestick of the Jews, "lost at the Ponte Molle, in Constantine's time." She imagines it found and relit: " 'As each branch is lighted, it shall have a differently colored lustre from the other six; and when all the seven are kindled, their radiance shall combine into the intense white light of truth.' "

The two part, and Hilda appears on the summit of her tower; "very lovely" is her aspect, "in the evening sunlight," which has "little further to do with the world . . .

save to fling a golden glory on Hilda's hair, and vanish."
From her height the sculptor looks "sad and dim" in the
"dusky street" below. Kenyon, looking upward, on his
part reflects: " 'How like a spirit she looks, aloft there,
with the evening glory round her head. . . . How far above
me! how unattainable! Ah, if I could lift myself to her
region! Or,—if it be not a sin to wish it,—would that I
might draw her down to an earthly fireside!' "

Later, discussing the crime of Donatello and Miriam,
Kenyon suggests that the verdict for them might be
"worthy of Death, but not unworthy of Love." Hilda is
less tolerant, "looking at the matter through the clear
crystal medium of her own integrity": " 'This thing, as
regards its causes, is all a mystery to me, and must remain
so. But there is, I believe, only one right and one wrong;
and I do not understand, and may God keep me from
ever understanding, how two things so totally unlike can
be mistaken for one another.' " Kenyon wants to "say
something more" but yields to the "gentle steadfastness"
with which Hilda declines to listen. She grows sad; the
discussion of "this one dismal topic" has set, "as it were,
a prison-door ajar, and allowed a throng of torturing
recollections to escape from their dungeons into the pure
air and white radiance of her soul."

She is, however, once more entangled, and plunged
physically, though not spiritually, into the darkness of
Miriam's affairs. Miriam has entrusted to her a mysterious
packet, which, "if unclaimed after a certain period," she is
to deliver to a specified address. The errand leads Hilda
into "the foulest and ugliest part of Rome" to "a confusion
of black and hideous houses, piled massively out of the

ruins of former ages." In this neighborhood, dirt is "every-where" and assumes "the guise of human life in the chil-dren that seemed to be engendered out of it." Their father is "the sun, and their mother—a heap of Roman mud." Hilda's ominous destination is "the paternal abode of Beatrice, the gloomy old palace of the Cencis," the true abode of dark complexities of sin and sorrow. And here she disappears from view.

On the same day Kenyon, unexpectedly disappointed when she fails to meet him in the galleries of the Vatican, where he has meant to declare his love, is approached by a masked penitent. As he presently realizes, it is Donatello who speaks to him "in a voice not unfamiliar . . . though rendered remote and strange by the guilty veil" through which it penetrates. The penitent's question, " 'Is all well with you, Signore?' " is not reassuring, and the encounter takes on "the sinister aspect of an omen." The sculptor is left disconsolate by Hilda's failure to meet him:

> It was hard, we must allow, to see the shadow of a wintry sunset falling upon a day that was to have been so bright. . . . So much had been anticipated from these now vanished hours, that it seemed as if no other day could bring back the same golden hopes.

A man of equable and judicious temperament, he seeks a remedy:

> In a case like this, it is doubtful whether Kenyon could have done a much better thing than he actually did, by going to dine at the Cafe Nuovo, and drinking a flask of Monte-fiascone; longing, the while, for a beaker or two of Don-

atello's Sunshine. It would have been just the wine to cure a lover's melancholy, by illuminating his heart with tender light and warmth, and suggestions of undefined hopes, too ethereal for his morbid humor to examine and reject them.

No true Sunshine being available, however, the expedient is not wholly successful.

Making his way through a "complication of narrow streets," he encounters Miriam in a carriage, who, like Donatello, asks, "'Is all well with you?'" Her dress, reminiscent of the gorgeous Zenobia's, is "richer than the simple garb" that she usually wears. She is wearing a gem which glimmers "with a clear, red lustre, like the stars in a southern sky." This jewel seems to be "an emanation of herself," as if all that is "passionate and glowing, in her native disposition," has "crystallized upon her breast" and is "just now scintillating more brilliantly than ever, in sympathy with some emotion of her heart." We know, however, that the jewel is also the emblem of her blood-guilt, a dark, equivocal treasure (Chapter XLIII, "The Extinction of a Lamp").

The lamp on Hilda's tower has gone out, since she is no longer there to tend it. Kenyon, left in much the same situation as Hilda's earlier ordeal of isolation, feels that a light has gone out, or at least is "ominously obscured," to which he owes whatever cheerfulness has "heretofore illuminated his cold, artistic life." The idea of Hilda has been "like a taper of virgin wax, burning with a pure and steady flame, and chasing away the evil spirits out of the magic circle of its beams." It has "darted its rays afar, and modified the whole sphere" in which Kenyon has his being. Now he finds himself "in darkness and astray."

How dreary is Rome, "when any gloom within the heart corresponds to the spell of ruin, that has been thrown over the site of ancient empire." The past lies very heavy here: "You look through a vista of century beyond century,—through much shadow, and a little sunshine. . . . Your own life is as nothing, when compared with that immeasurable distance; but still you demand, none the less earnestly, a gleam of sunshine, instead of a speck of shadow, on the step or two that will bring you to your quiet rest." (Chapter XLV, "The Flight of Hilda's Doves").

Relief, however, is at hand. The sculptor is mysteriously summoned outside the city gates, and sets forth on a "bright forenoon of February; a month in which the brief severity of a Roman winter is already past, and when violets and daisies begin to show themselves in spots favored by the sun" (Chapter XLVI, "A Walk on the Campagna"). In the country, "the warm rays of the sun" are "wholesome for him in body and soul." Accordingly, Donatello and Miriam, who come to meet him, bring reassurance about Hilda's safety (Chapter XLVII, "The Peasant and Contadina"). Of Miriam's and Donatello's tragedy, Miriam asks: " 'Was that very sin,—into which Adam precipitated himself and all his race,—was it the destined means by which, over a long pathway of toil and sorrow, we are to attain a higher, brighter, and profounder happiness, than our lost birthright gave?' "

It is carnival time, and "the stately avenue of the Corso" is peopled with "hundreds of fantastic shapes," some of which, the author says, probably represent the "mirth of ancient times, surviving through all manner of calamity, ever since the days of the Roman Empire. For a few afternoons of early spring, this mouldy gayety strays into the sunshine." To the worried Kenyon, on this occasion the Corso is "but a narrow and shabby street of decaying palaces; and even the long, blue streamer of Italian sky, above it, not half so brightly blue as formerly." If, however, "he could have beheld the scene with his clear, natural eyesight, he might still have found both merriment and splendor in it" (Chapter XLVIII, "A Scene in the Corso").

The story draws to an end, and the author advises his "gentle reader" to bear with its "romantic mysteries," in terms which remind us of Kenyon's reflections on the difference between the inside and the outside of stained-glass windows (Chapter L, "Miriam, Hilda, Kenyon, Donatello"). The devotee supplies from within the brightness of his faith:

> He is too wise to insist upon looking closely at the wrong side of the tapestry, after the right one has been sufficiently displayed to him, woven with the best of the artist's skill, and cunningly arranged with a view to the harmonious exhibition of its colors. If any brilliant, or beautiful, or even tolerable effects have been produced, this pattern of kindly readers will accept it at its worth.

A final retrospective scene is laid in the Pantheon, as most fitting, its "gray dome above, with its opening to the sky, as if heaven were looking down into the interior of this place of worship."

Kenyon remarks that " 'it is to the aperture in the dome —that great Eye, gazing heavenward—that the Pantheon owes the peculiarity of its effect.' " Hilda, the Sun Maiden, likes better "to look at the bright, blue sky. . . . It is very delightful, in a breezy day, to see the masses of white cloud float over the opening, and then the sunshine fall through it again, fitfully, as it does now. Would it be any wonder if we were to see angels hovering there, partly in and partly out, with genial, heavenly faces, not intercepting the light, but only transmuting it into beautiful colors?"

Kenyon propounds once more the problem of Sin, " 'which has educated Donatello, and elevated him. Is sin, then,—which we deem such a dreadful blackness in the universe,—is it, like sorrow, merely an element of human education, through which we struggle to a higher and purer state than we could otherwise have attained?' " But Hilda expresses such horror as to wound "the poor, speculative sculptor to the soul." In a passage that calls to mind the transcendental distinction between understanding and reason, understanding and the intellect abdicate before the absolute knowledge of reason's white light. As Kenyon pleads;

"The mind wanders wild and wide; and, so lonely as I live and work, I have neither pole-star above nor light of cottage-windows here below, to bring me home. Were you my guide, my counsellor, my inmost friend, with that white wisdom which clothes you as a celestial garment, all would go well."

As for the sad mystery, the questions remain unanswered: "For, what was Miriam's life to be? And where was Donatello? But Hilda had a hopeful soul, and saw sunlight on the mountain-tops."

VI. AFTERWORD

THE world, or the "reality," of Hawthorne's major romances is essentially solar, despite the "power of blackness" in it. It is a traditional cosmos consisting of heaven, earth, and hell, though whether heaven and hell are metaphors or objects is impossible to say. If they are objects, Hawthorne claims no precise or geographical knowledge of them; his sphere is earth, a mixed region of "care, and sorrow, and troubled joy." It is possible for the reader to interpret his regions of the supernatural and preternatural simply as psychological states or as purely dramatic images drawn from the beliefs of the characters the romancer has created. I personally cannot rid myself of a feeling that when a man talks of heaven and hell with some frequency heaven and hell are what he means. At any rate, "Middle Earth" is certainly the haunt and the main region of his song. Yet the other spheres continually impinge on Hawthorne's world; his sunlight is both natural and supernatural, as is his darkness.

Sunlight in Hawthorne's fiction has two poles, which as extremes have points of contact. Thus the "white radiance" that Kenyon invokes in *The Marble Faun*, the total and ineffable light of the divine, is the extreme opposite of the "broad and simple daylight" of its Preface, a light inimical to the effects of romance. Yet they are alike in being absolutes; and they are equally impossible to art, divinity as a white light being both too simple and too complex to image. As absolutes they represent the two opposite modes of reality, and the theoretical possibility of reconciling them, which Hawthorne momentarily touches in the "bright transparency" of the "Custom House" passage.

Intermediate stages are ambiguous, since Hawthorne uses the sun, in traditional fashion, both as the natural source of light and life and as the symbol of godhead, so that we have the "blessed sunshine" and the "benignant smile" of the Creator. To resort perforce to an unfortunate expression, interpretation will depend upon shading. Thus it is just to say that Hester seeks a natural redemption, Dimmesdale a supernatural one. But the two are almost interfused, not clearly separate. The light that surrounds Pearl is at one time too purely natural, at another all too heavenly, since neither is a safe resort for one who must live in the mixed world of humanity. Thus, too, the sunlight of Phoebe, the evanescent brightness of Priscilla, the white light of Hilda.

The consideration brings us to the relation between reality and romance. Hawthorne, it seems evident, saw this relationship clearly enough and yet was unwilling to accept it fully, so that his yearning for reality remained somewhat separate from his sense of art. It is customary to lament this gap, a breach attributed to his Puritanism, his urge toward didacticism. In dealing with his Prefaces, I have earlier suggested that he conceived of his two worlds of the Actual and the Imaginary too skeptically for his own artistic purposes. Yet, perhaps, since this division represented his deep belief and genuine cast of mind, it is an element of strength and vitality,—not a weakness at all, but the configuration of his art, the result of forcible stresses. Perhaps the world of his romances is formed, not mangled, by his sense of reality. The poignancy of the Borghese gardens, or of Blithedale in sun and shade, might not be possible without it.

The resolution of the conflict—if indeed Hawthorne really wished to resolve it—lies in the harmony of light and dark, the proportionateness and "keeping" that he everywhere envisioned. Traditionally enough, yet deeply and organically, his fundamental figure was pictorial. All values, all colors, light and darkness are interdependent, mutually supporting each other, but supported in turn by the absolute conceptions of pure light that stand at opposite extremes beyond the scope of the picture itself. Hester is defined by Dimmesdale and Chillingworth and Pearl, and each of them in turn is modified by the dark background of Puritan Boston. Phoebe is impossible without dark Hepzibah; Miriam depends upon the simpler colorations of Donatello, the model, and Hilda. The reality of Hawthorne's desire lies in the distinctness, the *realization*, which is also a necessary element of the picturesque.

INDEX

HAWTHORNE'S IMAGERY was set on the Linotype in eleven-point Janson, a revival of the sparkling seventeenth-century typeface cut by Anton Janson.

Chapter titles and initials are handset Centaur capitals, designed after classic Roman models by the celebrated American designer-printer, Bruce Rogers.

Ornaments are simple type rules of various weights, used to suggest the interplay of light and dark which is the theme of the book.

The paper on which this book is printed bears the watermark of the University of Oklahoma Press and is designed to have an effective life of over three hundred years.

THE UNIVERSITY OF OKLAHOMA PRESS

NORMAN